FROM THE STREET CORNER

TO THE CORNER OFFICE

ISBN: 1452838828
ISBN-13: 9781452838823
LCCN: 2010906147

From The Street Corner to The Corner Office

Michael J. Thomas

TABLE OF CONTENTS

About Author and Title

There are those who are to the manor born. Then there are guys like me. Far from the manor but closer to heaven, I was born and raised in Harlem, New York, circa 1950. My first known address was the Lincoln Projects, 2155 Madison Avenue, 135th Street, Apartment 11-H. That's the same Madison Avenue of advertising fame and fortune, located some sixty city blocks due south. Separating the two vastly different worlds was several trillion dollars and a landmark known as Central Park.

Despite this great cultural divide, I considered my world far more attractive. The streets of Harlem at the time of my youth were filled with a passing parade of colorful characters, generating a positive energy I quickly grew to love. What we lacked in cash, we made up for in cachet. Where else could you hang out on any given street corner and view the likes of Malcolm X, Martin Luther King Jr., Jackie Robinson, Willie Mays, Miles Davis, Sugar Ray Robinson, Muhammad Ali, or Adam Clayton Powell all doing their thing? What great theatre! It didn't matter whether you agreed with their particular brand of religion, politics, or lifestyle. Instinctively, you could tell that these were people of great substance, people who were making a difference in the world as well as in our neighborhoods. These were people you somehow wanted to emulate.

Harlem was also home to its fair share of gypsies, tramps, and thieves. I tried hard to distance myself from the scoundrels, though it wasn't always easy. That's because more than a few of these social misfits and innocent victims of circumstance were close friends and distant relatives. But for the most part, Harlem was home to decent, hard-working, middle-class, low-income families trying mightily to realize The American Dream, with precious little time to sleep. Ours was the sort of household in which I was fortunate and glad to be a part.

My father was a tool and die maker whose winsome personality proved to be his real trade in life. He had a booming voice that would wake the day and a laugh that made you smile. When he walked into a room, you knew it, and when he left, you felt a sense of deep despair. I was proud to call him Dad and, in turn, felt the need to take pride in myself.

My mom's real trade in life was that of a devoted wife and loving mother. She was the heart and soul of the Thomas household, without whom there would have been no sense of family. She cooked, cleaned, and worked out-side the home. But most of all, she taught us what it meant to love and be loved.

Rounding out the family of four was an older brother who proved to be my guardian angel, guiding light, and very best friend in life. He provided a safety net that allowed me to be the precocious little brother without fear, trepidation, or reprisal. I took risks for which he would often pay the price, and while vexed, seldom did he bat an eye. With big bro' providing protective cover, I was empowered to challenge life at a tender age in ways he never could. It's a favor I can never repay.

Such was the manor to which I was born. As a result, I grew to be cocky, self-confident, and terribly self-assured, albeit "without a pot to piss in or the window to throw it out of," to quote a mother's phrase. By the time I fled the family nest at the age of twenty-one, I possessed little more than debt, a college degree, and the dogged determination to succeed at something other than nothing. A twenty-seven-year career in Corporate America provided an unexpected means to an unlikely end, so that, by the time I was thrown from the corporate nest, I was forty-nine years old, retired, and financially set for life.

This was a fate I never saw coming. My initial goal in life was to become a world-noted psychologist, with hopes of leaving the world a better place in which to live, while at the same time making lots of cash. But long before securing the necessary credentials, I got married and started a family, which forced me to pursue gainful employment way ahead of my intended schedule. A career in Corporate America was the furthest thing from my mind but the closest thing at hand to serve my immediate needs. Without benefit of a business curriculum, MBA, or comparable socio-economic breeding, I made the transition from asphalt jungle to corporate jungle, with little more to guide me than native intelligence, street smarts, and a liberal arts education. Despite this handicap, I managed to move from the ranks of entry-level employee to that of corporate officer. In addition to the loot, I have the scars and stripes to prove it.

From the Street Corner chronicles my improbable personal journey from Point A (the street corner) to Point B (the corner office) in hopes that the reader can relate in some meaningful way. Race, color, creed; age, sex, marital status; birthday, birthplace, and birthrights are to some extent relevant, but not nearly as important as the things we all share in common. This conversation has more to do with mind and body, heart and soul, spirit and sense of self. It speaks to survival skills and coping with your environment, no matter where it finds you, how you happened to get there, or what it feels like to be there.

In setting forth this material, I make no claim to be right or theoretically correct. Indeed, I am no stranger to human error or mistakes. I have experienced failure in my life, both personally and professionally, on more than one occasion. I've been divorced, demoted, and dismissed, in each case against my will. I've been dishonored, disillusioned, and dismayed, in each case by things of my own doing. Still, I have yet to meet the man with whom I'd be willing to trade places, and it's highly unlikely I ever will. Rightly or wrongly, I have come to the conclusion that being the best you can be is damn near as good as it gets. The only thing better is helping others come to the same conclusion, which is precisely what inspired me to put forth this effort.

There are no silver bullets, secret formulas, or get-rich-quick schemes to be had here. If that's your hustle, you're better off wishing on stars, chasing moonbeams, or searching for sunken gold. What you have here, instead, is a digest of my honest impressions on what it takes to succeed in Corporate America. Object lessons deal with how to socialize, politicize, and patronize within the corporate environment. This compilation of dos and don'ts may or may not prove to be useful to the reader. All I know for sure is that these very same object lessons have converged in a way that put me in a place others seem to envy. Readers are encouraged to challenge this material and take advantage of only those things that appear to be worthwhile.

CORPORATE AMERICA DEFINED

Before turning your attention to the wisdom of my experience, we should get clear on what Corporate America is, who the players are, and what generally goes on inside. It's no secret that Corporate America is the bastion of capitalism, the place where big business dwells. Principal tenants are commonly referred to as "Fortune 500" companies. These companies usually dominate within their industry, from petroleum, to finance, to pharmaceuticals. They set the pace for others to follow by way of vision, innovation, design, and execution. While business pursuits may vary, the nature of all business is ever constant. Corporate America exists for the sole purpose of making money, period. Companies that fail to make money, incrementally and in perpetuity, will surely be bought, sold, or die. Critical measures of success include revenues, profits, and, ultimately, shareholder value.

The role Corporate America plays in shaping the world we live in is breathtaking. Practically speaking, it drives the global economy, generating trillions in revenue, billions in profit, and tons of shareholder value. Politically speaking, it's our de facto fourth branch of government, the best that money can buy, so to speak, wielding much the same power as judges, legislators, and presidents. Why, the whole notion of "land of the free and home of the brave" is primarily funded by what occurs in Corporate America, so much so that it is hard to imagine a civilized society without it. It takes a free-enterprise system to make for our democratic way of life. That, taxes, and apparently, war.

Speaking of war, it takes an army of people to wage a corporate campaign. Accordingly, Corporate America is the place where millions of Americans report to work daily. Surprisingly enough, Kelly Services is the second-largest American employer, with 750,000 people on its books. Not so surprisingly, Wal-Mart is the number-one employer, with 1.8 million people on its payroll.

The remaining eight members on the top-ten list of American employers, based on *The Almanac of American Employers, 2008,* are McDonald's, United Parcel Service, IBM, Home Depot, Target, Citigroup, General Electric, and AT&T, in that order. Between them, they employ more than five million people, while the other forty of the fifty largest employers have more than twelve million people on their payrolls. Now, these companies and their employee counts will surely change over time. But no matter which companies rank as the top fifty employers, they will necessarily need a militia!

Much like in the military, rank has its privileges in Corporate America. The chairman of the board is commander-in-chief, followed by the chief executive officer, the chief financial officer, the chief operating officer, and a whole host of chief petty officers, to boot. This group represents less than 1 percent of the total employee population, but to them go the fortunes of war. Captains of industry, perched atop their organizations, can earn hundreds of millions of dollars, annually, betwixt and between salary, bonuses, perquisites, and stock option grants. From there, the wealth trickles down through every layer of the organization. The closer you are to the top, the more you get wet. When it's all said and done, employees hold positions that extend from the mailroom to the boardroom, with pay grades that range from the ridiculous to the sublime, while working anywhere from "9 to 5" to "24/7."

The chain of command in Corporate America is set forth by way of organizational charts, clearly defined reporting relationships, rules, regulations, policies, and procedures. Marching orders come from corporate headquarters. Field marshals execute battle plans that are designed to capture enemy territory. Said differently, managers execute marketing strategies that are designed to capture market share. Esprit de corps is driven through the ranks by way of mission statements and vision statements; insignias and logos; mottos, oaths, and slogans. An occasional kick in the ass further helps to reinforce corporate goals and objectives.

But I digress. Whether a career in Corporate America is tantamount to a military exercise or not is not the point. What's important to note is the depth, breath, and scope of opportunity that exists within Corporate America. The potential to engage in meaningful work while generating wealth and the peace of mind that comes with it is real. And humble beginnings need not limit one's ability to achieve. Aside from common sense, a command of the language, and a firm grasp of math, all that's required to advance through the ranks is a fundamental understanding of the corporate culture and the know-how to make it work for you, as opposed to you merely working for it. The armed services analogy simply provides a practical frame of reference from whence to draw critical points of distinction not readily apparent.

Belying the outward appearance of civility, things can get pretty nasty in the trenches of Corporate America, especially for those of you who would seek to scale the corporate ladder. Thin-skinned people need not apply. It can be an "every man for himself," "dog-eat-dog," "watch your back" kind of world, much lonelier at the bottom than it is at the top. Friendly competition begets rivalry, which begets backstabbing and betrayal—all within the blink of an eye. Corporate soldiers who live to brag about services rendered with pride, passion, and a pocketful of money do so only after having faced a wide variety of great danger.

The war games played in Corporate America are more like mind games or bloodless coups, predicated on man's inherent need to divide and, ultimately, conquer. Someone has to win, someone has to lose, and to the victor go the spoils. Pitched battles and the threat of doom are to be expected within the corporate environment. Going for the gusto minimally requires mental toughness, blind ambition, and guts. Good corporate soldiers bound for glory must be committed to a long and treacherous journey. Win, lose, or draw, no one escapes unscathed.

Check your backpack before breaking camp in Corporate America, as you will need the following equipment by journey's end: nerves of steel, the patience of Job, steadfast perseverance, the ability to negotiate an often lopsided battlefield, a knack for building alliances and operating within the framework of a team while maintaining your own identity, interpersonal skills that allow you to suffer fools gladly while gaining the respect of intelligent men, an awareness of your limits, the strength to overcome them, and finally, an awfully good sense of humor.

These interpersonal skills are developed over time, starting at a very early age. It's the stuff that builds character, which proudly says to the world, "what you see is what you get"! Harlem proved to be fertile ground upon which to sow these seeds of self-determination. It just goes to show you that "God works in mysterious ways; His wonders never cease"!

Understanding the
Corporate Culture

Having broached the subject of a higher authority, the following observation seems in order. Nowhere is the separation of church and state more pronounced than in Corporate America. The only hard evidence suggesting a link between the two are the words "In God We Trust" emblazoned on coins in 1909 and on bills since 1957. That notable exception aside, it is safe to assume that in religion and business "never the twain shall meet," unless you consider silent prayer, taking the Lord's name in vain, or exclaiming "holy shit!" in the face of shrinking profits a proclamation of faith. The only Almighty to be worshipped in Corporate America is, without question, the almighty dollar. It's the one common denominator that transcends denomination, above which there is no other. Amen.

CEOs are, in effect, modern-day messiahs, charged with the responsibility of amassing shareholder value or wealth on behalf of the privileged few who already have too much. Their collective need for "mo' money, mo' money, mo' money" is everlasting. Lest I give you the impression that I hold corporate titans in contempt, I should hasten to assure you that I don't. Capital barons like Bill Gates, Warren Buffett, and the Waltons carry on in the fine tradition of their legendary forefathers, men like Andrew Carnegie, J. P. Morgan, and the Rockefellers.

Were it not for these storied soldiers of fortune, American values would be terribly hard to come by, in far more ways than one. The Kozlowskis, Lays, and Madoffs of the world represent the worst of their kind and should be thought of as fiscal thugs. They and others like them will go down in history as being what Arianna Huffington refers to as "Pigs at the Trough," people whose avarice and greed led them astray, absent sight of the greater good. Damn them and their evil deeds that bring shame to a noble cause.

Upon entering the ranks of Corporate America, I, too, became a soldier of fortune. But the rich legacy of my legendary forefathers was totally lost on me. What struck me most was the paltry sum of my annual starting salary. At $8,400, I held no hope of becoming either rich or famous. Such woefully puny wages convinced me that I was, forevermore, part of the petty proletariat. Had I known then what I know now, I might have seen things differently. With 20/20 hindsight, I realize that I could have easily fixed my gaze on becoming chairman of the board.

I'm embarrassed to admit that I didn't get the big picture. As a new kid on the corporate block, my field of vision barely extended beyond the neighborhood of my desk. My only associates were the people who sat on either side of me. As a group, we were perched near the bottom of a corporate ladder that supported thousands of employees, on countless rungs above us, and a scant few down below. That being the case, I was badly disillusioned. I made the horrible mistake of allowing a *Dilbert*-like position, and modest starting salary to negatively affect my point of view. By virtue of an urban upbringing, I should have known better than to get my dauber down.

For some ungodly reason, I entered Corporate America with eyes wide shut and head hung low. The last thing I want for you is to make that same mistake. If you haven't done so already, take the time to examine your company's organizational chart. It's the best way to get a good read on the lay of the land and your proper fit within the grand scheme of things.

THE ORGANIZATIONAL CHART

Any company worth its salt will have organizational charts. Check with human resources or the personnel department. If they don't have any, take some from a company that does, or better yet, make one up. Organizational charts are universal in nature; if you've seen one, you've seen them all. Start at the top of the chart and work your way down until you have accounted for every position within the firm, not the least of which will be your own. Break the total employee population into six separate and distinct groups, to wit: senior, upper, middle, and lower management, bureaucrats, and last but not least, support staff. Groupings should be broad enough to accommodate everyone. For the sake of this discussion, let's use the following example:

SENIOR MANAGEMENT

This small, loosely knit group includes the CEO, the president, and all the president's men. They are few in number, usually five or less, but together they constitute an inner circle which is singularly responsible for the company's welfare. The fact that they seldom sing from the same hymnal should come as no surprise, for they are in pursuit of their own agendas. It's the job of the CEO to keep shareholders and/or principal owners content. The only legitimate way to accomplish this is by growing the business, profitably. But, alas, these two objectives are often diametrically opposed. What's good for growth isn't always good for profit. What's good for profit isn't always good for growth. If the CEO knows what's good for him or her, he or she will order the president to select a crusader for each cause and let the two warriors fight it out. And fight they will, with the eventual winner becoming heir apparent. The CEO is also well advised to have a chief financial officer who can cook the books, a chief investment officer who can make something out of nothing, and a general counsel who can make wrong seem right without compunction.

Upper Management

This is a slightly larger group that takes its lead from the inner circle. They may not have as much power, but they certainly have plenty of clout. Their job is to create subgroups within a group, thereby driving the corporate mandate of profitable growth throughout the rest of the organization. Major corporations have anywhere from ten to twenty group vice presidents, and they, in turn, will have at least two or three vice presidents reporting to them. More than fifty upper managers can make for a top-heavy organization, with lines of authority that begin to blur.

Middle Management

These people actually execute corporate plans and strategy. It is their job to bridge the gap between what senior management wants to do and how best to get it done. It's where you first begin to notice just how much shit can run downhill. They number in the hundreds, with titles that include assistant vice president, director, and department manager. Most middle managers operate on frontlines outside the "Ivory Tower," where they can see the world for what it is.

LOWER MANAGEMENT

Lower management or supervisors are the greatest in number with the least amount of power. They must do what they are told to do without asking too many questions. They are also expected to keep their subordinates in line, which is often akin to the blind leading the blind. When things don't go as planned, lower management will usually take the fall. All of this goes a long way to explain why supervisors can be such royal pains in the ass. With their jobs on the line and seemingly nowhere to hide, they probably feel as if they have no choice.

BUREAUCRATS

Bureaucrats are the elder statesmen of an organization. Given their years of experience and technical expertise, these people either know, or think they know, more about what's going on than any other group. They require very little supervision but don't necessarily make for good managers. For safety's sake, they would prefer to be a source of power behind the seat. These people are called analysts, specialists, technicians, and inside and outside consultants.

SUPPORT STAFF

Support staff is a slick euphemism for grunts. Otherwise known as the rank and file, support staff members constitute more than 90 percent of the employee population. They line up behind lower management and perform the daily, routine tasks that bring a company to life. These are the people who meet the marketplace face-to-face. If for no other reason, we should call them representatives. You have accounting reps, sales reps, marketing reps, and so on. The most common of all reps is the customer service rep. More than any other group, this dedicated "house of representatives," along with their companion backroom operators, drive customer satisfaction, which is the DNA of profitable growth. In light of their needful efforts, you'd think that their lot in life would be a whole lot better.

Let's put that bit of irony aside for the moment for the sake of staying on point. Now that we know where everyone in the organization is situated, we should consider how he or she got there. Such things don't happen by chance. Some people *work to live* while others *live to work*. The difference between these two dispositions can be substantial and often dictates where you end up on the organizational chart.

Working to Live vs. Living to Work

People who work to live are in it for the money, by and large, to keep from starving. They will trade a GED, high school diploma, or undergraduate degree in exchange for an entry-level position. Little or no experience is required of them. Happy to have a job, they operate on the basis of "another day, another dollar." What matters most to them are steady work, hourly wages, and a paycheck. Whether the company makes money is of less concern than their own financial well-being. As long as they show up for work and do a good job, these people expect to get paid. They also expect two to five weeks of paid vacation, a pension, generous company benefits (i.e., health care), and annual raises that outpace the rate of inflation. This is as good as it gets for people who work to live and as good as it needs to be. When you think about it, that's not all bad.

People who live to work are also in it for the money, but money alone is not enough. These people need power, as well, and they are more than willing to do whatever it takes to get their fill of both. They are your garden-variety overachievers, control freaks, and egomaniacs. A degree in "BS" is standard equipment. Some come fully loaded with an MBA, PhD, or both. Their entry-level positions are simply stepping stones, which typically lead to bigger and better things. They will put the company's welfare above their own, feeling certain that to do so is in their best interest. As they move through the ranks, they will relocate around the country if not the globe, uprooting family ties along the way. Each new job demands more of their time, which further displaces the family unit. Be that as it may, people who live to work will not be denied until, career-wise, they can scale to great heights or die trying.

To further distinguish between these two dispositions, I ask you to consider this. It's been said that the chicken is *involved* with making breakfast, vis-à-vis its egg. The pig, however, is *committed* to making breakfast, vis-à-vis its bacon. It would be unfair to suggest that people who work to live are chickens or that people who live to work are pigs. The analogy, however, has some merit. People who work to live are *involved* with making money. People who live to work are *committed* to making money, and gaining power in the process. Neither disposition is inherently better than the other. It's more a dictate of will and skill, and your threshold for pain and suffering. The question you have to ask yourself is this: what do I need from my job to be satisfied, and what price am I willing to pay?

Most corporate soldiers have the wherewithal to earn a decent living without committing much more than time and energy. That's the beauty of the system. Thirty years of continuous hard labor can yield a six-digit income, 401K cash, and a retirement package worth more than a million bucks. But only a fraction of corporate soldiers are up to earning a living while engaged in a power struggle. Scaling the corporate ladder takes you out of the comfort zone. The rewards are greater, but so is the risk. And if your grasp somehow exceeds your reach, you can blow the whole kit and caboodle. Within the context of an organizational chart, people who work to live are best suited to support staff and bureaucrat positions. People who live to work are best suited to management positions. There is nothing to prevent you from changing your disposition, but absent the appropriate mind-set, you are fighting a losing battle.

Scaling the Corporate Ladder and the Good Old Boy Network

People who work to live are less affected, but people who live to work can forget about scaling the corporate ladder without making the proper management connections. This is how many MBAs and PhDs manage to get a head start. Most have studied the exploits of corporate bigwigs. Some are acquainted on a first-name basis. It behooves you to get acquainted, as well, even if from afar. Start by gathering intelligence on people in high places throughout the entire organization, as best you can. Think of it as an exercise in due diligence. Your company's annual report is required reading. Senior management profiles are usually contained therein. Look for things like educational background, age, and years of experience. You will notice that in addition to scholarship, experience and loyalty are not without reward.

According to a report by Wendy Todaro appearing in *Forbes Magazine*, chief executive officers at America's one hundred largest companies fit the following profile: "15 of the 100 joined their companies directly after graduating from college. Thirty-five started their professional careers at the company they currently lead. Four began their careers with the companies they are now in charge of after leaving and returning. Thirty-one have been with only one other company, twelve with two, and thirteen with two or more." In this same report, according to Drake Beam Morin, a New York-based consultancy firm, "51% of U.S. CEO's have spent 20 or more years working for the companies they now head. Across all industries, the average CEO is 50 years old upon taking office."

Not that all CEOs will fit this profile, but as a general rule, senior managers are seasoned veterans who have fought the good fight over a decent amount of time while climbing atop the corporate heap. Given your heap, you should know these people and how they came to power. Any manager who has ever worked for a senior manager should also be taken into account. Throw in managers who have worked for managers who have worked for senior managers and what you end up with is a management hierarchy within the overall chain of command. Behold, "the good old boy network."

Senior managers are connected to certain upper managers, who, in turn, are connected to certain middle managers, and so on down the line. It's critically important for you to discern these ties, because scaling the corporate ladder is all about doing your job in ways that gain the favor of connected managers. Gaining the favor of connected managers is how you become part of the good old boy network. Becoming part of the good old boy network is how you get promoted.

We are entering the realm of corporate politics, where management careers are won and lost. Doing a good job is not nearly enough. The hallmark of any Fortune 500 company is to be stockpiled with upwardly mobile managers who can get the job done, anytime, any place, anywhere. This makes for stiff competition when vying for promotional opportunities. There will always be someone with job-related skills on par with the best you have to offer. For you to think otherwise would be capriciously naive. What lifts you above the maddening crowd is political acumen. Highly skilled managers who are politically weak will, invariably, get lost in the crowd.

CORPORATE POLITICS

The art or science of politics as defined by Webster's dictionary is *"the total complex of relations between people, concerned with winning and holding power."* That said, it seems to me that politicians and corporate soldiers share a common fate. Trying to get elected is not unlike trying to get promoted. The grassroots support of minions is important, but at the end of the day, you'll need the endorsement of the establishment before moving to higher ground. This political reality further underscores the power of the good old boy network, particularly in Corporate America, where the only votes that count belong to them.

There are some very bright people in Corporate America who have the crazy idea that they can move to higher ground without becoming politically active. That's like running for public office without getting out the vote. You can't possibly expect people to render power and follow your lead until you enlist their support and trust. The best way to achieve this goal is by what I call *working the crowd.* In the course of doing an exemplary job, you need to shake hands, slap backs, and mix and mingle with a cross-section of good old boys on both sides of the corporate aisle (growth and profit). This is an ongoing process which, when properly applied, builds a bipartisan network of corporate constituency.

Let's face it: brains and good looks can only get you so far. Good old boy (and girl) constituents are the political brawn behind any successful campaign. At any given point in your career, *who you know* will be of equal or greater value than *what you know*. In fairness to crazies, it's easy to understand how the political process could put off intelligent folk. Following the lead of some chosen few may not always seem to be the smart way to go. There are good old boys who are about to lose their power. Other good old boys don't know how to use their power. Then you have the good old boys who don't deserve their power. How they came to power in the first place is beyond comprehension. But if wielding power of your own is the primary objective, you must yield to those who are currently in command. People unwilling to respect authority are unlikely to ever possess it.

Rank has its privileges in Corporate America and it's been like that since time immemorial. Regardless of whether superiors are worthy of respect, don't let foolish pride or a bloated sense of self preempt your ability to placate the powers that be. That's what I would call a losing proposition. A win-win proposition is more what you're looking for. Paying tribute to the people in positions of power is the essence of playing the game. Failure to abide by this corporate protocol is political suicide.

The name of the game is serving many masters for the sake of advancing your own career. Since it's their house and their money, you must play the game by company rules.

The ante on the table is your paycheck. Good old boys are in the pit. To up your ante, you need their approval, which comes at a certain price. All you have to raise is service at their pleasure. From time to time, they will impose upon you in ways that are sure to make you rather uneasy. But their blatant calls shouldn't prompt your fold if kissing a little ass can turn the trick.

CORPORATE POLITICS AND THE ART OF KISSING ASS

I am reluctant to address such a touchy subject. The import, however, forces my nervous hand. We live in a gritty world filled with gritty issues, and it just so happens that this is one of them. Call me crude, but what I would like to do is get you comfortable with the idea of kissing ass. To reach this higher level of conscientiousness, I must ask you to keep an open mind. If, at the end of my deliberations, you are not on board, one of two things is undeniably true. Either I have botched an attempt to advance my position, or you have no business working in Corporate America.

Kissing ass, in its purest form, is nothing more than a sacrifice you are willing to make on behalf of someone you truly care about or whom you need to truly care about you. Random, gratuitous ass kissing, by contrast, is nothing short of a sacrilege. People who would take this awful approach are called sycophants, which is a fancy word for *ass kissers*. The term *yes men* also comes to mind. The difference between what I preach and what they practice is the difference between method and madness. Done with decorum, kissing ass is a good thing. I can think of no better way to get the favorable attention of the significant others in my life. And once I get their attention, I try to give them ample reason to want to kiss my ass in return. In political terms, it's called an aye for an aye. In practical terms, it's called doing what you have to do in order to get what you want.

Haven't you ever done a good deed for someone in hopes that he or she would return the favor? Gild the lily if you like, but that's what I call kissing ass! I can remember plying this simple trade as far back as my early childhood. Whether it was fixing and serving my parents breakfast in bed, running errands for neighbors, or polishing the teacher's apple, I gladly puckered up, fully expecting a quid pro quo. Why, I've kissed the asses of people whose names I didn't know. Absent any guarantees, more often than not, I got what I bargained for.

When you are involved in a relationship, personally or professionally, have a vested interest in nurturing that relationship, and have the opportunity to prove your best intentions, I'd say the "moons" are perfectly aligned. The time is so right to show how much you care. Currying the favor of kinfolk is relatively easy, as compared to doing the same for relative unknowns. Don't let bloodlines confuse the issue, because that would be the kiss of death. You will never make it big in Corporate America without answering the call to booty. Good old boys are obliged to heed the call, and they expect no less from you. No one connected to the network is exempt, not even the chairmen of the boards. They must fawn over a board of directors, any one of whom may have the ability to turn their world topsy-turvy. Kissing ass is, therefore, a necessary evil that should be kept in proper perspective.

Think back to your college days when students pledged via kissing ass over the course of an entire semester. Crossing the burning sands to become part of an inner circle made the sacrifice seem worthwhile. It works the same way in Corporate America. The good old boy network is like a mega frat that places comparable demands on your loyalty and commitment. This stands to reason when you consider the fact that the corporate fraternity plays a vital role in putting a roof over your head, food on the table, and those designer clothes on your back. That's more than you can say for Deltas or Kappas, and best of all, there's no hazing involved.

For those of you who can't take being humiliated, feel free to stand at ease while on the job. Kissing ass is nothing to be ashamed of in the halls of Corporate America. All that's required is getting busy on the job, in ways that others can't or won't. Start by doing the little things, like coming in early, staying late, and assuming more responsibility. Continue putting forth that extra effort by striving to outperform your peer group in ways that can be fiscally measured. When you productively raise the level of competition, corporate profits will rise with the tide. You may not consider this as kissing ass, but trust me, the good old boys do. They would call it "walking the walk," and I see no shame in that game.

Walking the walk lets the company know that you are eager to expand its horizons. After all, that's why they hired you. When applying for the job, you vowed such devotion out of the fear that if you didn't, they wouldn't hire you. And you were right! Once you are on the payroll, the company expects you to honor your words. Making good on job-related favors is an implicit part of that deal. What's done of your own volition is duly noted, but markers are made by coming to the aid of a colleague's cry for help. These markers could prove invaluable as you strive to advance your position. Never mind who's asking or what they would have you do, assuming it's legal. The fact that you are *there for them* may someday work to *your advantage*.

There's walking the walk, and then there's "talking the talk." Kissing ass contemplates both. In addition to doing what needs to be done, you should know what to say and how to say it. One without the other, at best, is no better than a half-assed smack. Talking the talk lets the company brass know that you are well equipped to speak their language. It tickles their fancy and teases their brains, which allows you to command their attention. Remember, good old boys have great big egos, and nothing gives them greater pleasure than having those egos stroked. Small talk, shoptalk, and sweet talk put you within "stroking" distance.

Small talk is the art of casual conversation that can establish a rapport with total strangers. Since good old boys like to dominate a conversation, it pays to let them do so. It also pays to have well-informed opinions before adding your two cents' worth. Although not a formal part of the job description, your obligation in Corporate America is to stay on top of current events. That's why God created *The Wall Street Journal*, *The New York Times*, and *USA Today*. These publications provide a common frame of reference, which makes them required reading. It's not necessary to read each one from cover to cover, just front-page stories in every section. Anything else you need to know can be gleaned from the local news, ESPN, and Al Gore's Internet.

Shoptalk is a meatier brand of conversation that gives good old boys something to work with. In terms of the natural flow of conversation, it carries on from where small talk leaves off. After establishing a rapport with good old boys, what remains is to earn their respect. To do that, you need to be just as well-informed when talking business as you are when talking trash. The company has an annual plan, which includes rate of growth, profit, and return on equity. Be prepared to discuss how your assignment fits this mission, in terms of year-to-date results. You should also have a solid grasp of the industry trends as they relate to the aforementioned. This is where trade publications come in handy. The goal is not to be a know-it-all, because no one likes a smart-ass. But when you can elevate the level of shoptalk without being obnoxious, good old boys are going to sit up and take note.

Sweet talk is the art of conversation that has less to do with substance than form. It essentially sets a pleasant tone for stuff that comes flying out of your mouth. Affirmation and confirmation are the key components of sweet talk. Together, they create an atmosphere wherein your colleagues can find self-esteem. Affirmation is the voice of positive feedback that gives credit where credit is due. Confirmation is the voice of a positive mental attitude that values the opinion of others. It's awfully hard not to like someone who entreats you to express yourself while patting you on the back. That's the subtle beauty of sweet talk. On the surface, sweet talk is incredibly cheap but priceless in terms of fostering a mood for more substantive conversation.

So there you have it: my case for kissing ass, and I trust you can get over the hump. Such things are done for your own good, more so than for the sake of others. It's easier to scale the corporate ladder when the people around you are inclined to clear a path. Walking the walk and talking the talk should be inclination enough. If you remain unconvinced that kissing ass is right for you, I urge you to go into sales. Most jobs in Corporate America require teamwork, which puts a premium on kissing ass. A sales job, however, allows for greater independence. As long as you hit production targets, co-workers have no choice but to cut you some slack. The catch-22 is dealing with a handful of customers who'll want you to kiss their asses!

Regardless of what you do for a living, someone's ass will be in your face. Should making money and gaining power be of consequence, the onus is on you to make ends meet. Kissing ass is nothing more than commissioned acts that conveniently serve that purpose. And if you're worried about what your cronies think of you, I beg you not to be stupid. Good old boys are the ones you need to worry about, starting with your boss.

You've Got to Love
Your Boss

It occurs to me that boss is a four-letter word, which when spelled backward is "double SOB." That in no way gives you the right to curse their utter existence. Bosses are descendants of the CEO, and it's to your everlasting advantage to treat them with respect. More than anyone in the organization, bosses hold your immediate fate in the palm of their sweaty little hands. Unless under contract, you work "at will" in Corporate America. Given this arrangement, bosses are within their legal right to fire you, anytime they please. Problems that exist between you and the boss are, therefore, problems you can't afford. "Jacks don't beat kings" was how my father put it. Crossing swords with the boss over an extended period of time will probably find you being hoisted by your own petard.

This is far more power than any one person should have, which might explain why we take perverse pleasure in railing against authority. If I had a penny for every potshot taken at the boss, I'd have more dollars than Bill, meaning Gates, which at last count was around sixty billion. Say what you want, but trashing the boss is conduct unbecoming. Over the course of my career, I had thirty different bosses, including twenty-eight white males, one black male, and one black female. Among these were several bigots. All were a part of the network. Not one of them was perfect. I admired a few, was cordial with all, and only wished one dead. Without taking stock of my own shortcomings, it was easy to pick them apart. But after my sniping, the fact remained unchanged that the boss was still the boss.

By virtue of power inherited, bosses live to be loved, not scorned. Even when they piss you off, bite your tongue and forever hold your peace. Bosses are above recrimination and words will never harm them. Instead of ragging on the boss, you should devote yourself to helping the boss look good. Show me a boss and I'll show you someone in need of a right-hand man, someone he or she can count on and trust. That someone should be you. This is not to say that you should force your affection on the boss, or worse yet, sell your soul to the devil. But to have a ghost's chance in hell of getting promoted, the boss needs to see you as an ally.

This is what I call "joining forces" with the boss, which goes way beyond your job well done. In addition to carrying your own weight with flair, get your ass in gear to share the boss's load. It doesn't matter whether you hate his guts or worship the ground she walks on, this is business; it's not personal. Courting the boss is standard operating procedure when it comes to advancing your cause. Your approach should be slow and steady, but direct and to the point. Let bosses know that you can best serve their interests once you have a feel for what's required of them. The boss is under different pressure to perform, but your jobs are interrelated. When you take the initiative to measure up to his or her standards, it logistically puts you in position to follow in his or her footsteps. What I am telling you is what my mother told me. She said, "In order to get where you're going, son, you have to act like you're already there."

Now, if the boss is reluctant to take you under his or her wing, back off before push comes to shove. There are other forces within the organization that can guide you through the land of *bilk* and *money*.

Mentors, Sponsors, and Monsters

According to Greek mythology, Mentor was a trusted counselor to Odysseus with ties to Athena and Telemachus. In the workplace, mentors are teachers with ties to the good old boy network. A mentor's stock in trade is useful information, and all you need to do is lend an ear. They can advise you on matters pertaining to the job as well as your personal development. Mentors have been down the road you travel while managing to enjoy a measure of success. That they are willing to help others achieve a measure of success is what makes them such a precious commodity.

Potential mentors should be easy to spot. They are the people within your division that others respect, due to their performance, both past and present. Although mentors may not occupy the captain's chair, they are informal leaders, nonetheless. When the going gets tough, mentors get going and can be counted on to rise above the fray. The only agenda that a mentor has is what best serves the company. This pretty much makes them indispensable as far as the boss is concerned. In fact, the nature of their relationship often places them second in command.

Mentors will tell you what you need to know, which won't always be what you want to hear. Fortunately for you, they are secure in their positions, unafraid of stepping on your toes. The best of mentors may occasionally acknowledge your strengths, but it's your weaknesses that draw their attention. The advice they offer often comes in the form of constructive criticism. Understandably, no one likes to be criticized; however, in the face of the mentors' friendly fire, you had better learn to bite their bullets. What they are trying to do, not unlike drill sergeants, is make you more fit for duty.

Ideally, you should have lots of mentors, to include the bosses, their bosses, peers, and subordinates. If this is more than you can hope for, then take what you can get. The ultimate goal is to create a network of bona fide associates who can provide you with 360 degrees of useful feedback. There's a wealth of information to be gathered here which, ordinarily, doesn't cost you a dime. Mentors give freely of themselves, expect nothing in return, and come with no strings attached.

Sponsors should not be confused with mentors. They look like mentors, and sometimes they act like mentors, but sharp contrasts exist between the two. These contrasts shouldn't be lost on you, because if they are, you will live to regret it. The single most important distinction between mentors and sponsors has to do with their access to power—that is to say, the power to promote. Mentors have very little power in this regard. All they can do is to promote within their unit. Beyond that, mentors are powerless, except for their ties to the good old boy network.

Sponsors, on the other hand, are the backbone of the good old boy network. They control divisions, which consist of many units, and have the power to promote up and down the line. Rarely will you work directly for a sponsor, especially in the early stages of your career. Sponsors are commonly two bosses removed from your current position, but you don't get promoted without their okay. As far as helping you move through the ranks is concerned, a single sponsor is worth a squadron of mentors.

Another distinction between mentors and sponsors has to do with their disposition. What a mentor has to offer comes straight from the heart; there's just no other way to explain it. When you ask for help, they are willing to oblige; when you ignore their advice, they grin and bear it. When you stumble and fall while on basic maneuvers, they will pick you up and dust you off. As long as you are making steady progress, mentors are likely to forgive your transgressions. While mentors may be qualified to show you the ropes, they don't share your accountabilities. And if, by chance, you were to ever crash and burn, there's never any skin off their backs. Methinks mentors can afford to "have a heart," which is far more than can be said for sponsors.

Sponsors are not predisposed to having a heart, and should you beg their indulgence, they will laugh in your face. Sponsors are all about getting results that allow the company to prosper. The extent to which you can help them realize their schemes is often the extent to which they give a damn about you. Cold, perhaps, but it makes perfect sense. Sponsors didn't get to be sponsors by making a lot of mistakes. And they won't remain sponsors for very long by associating with people who do. In order to hit and stay on a sponsor's radar screen, you need to become a zealot on behalf of his or her interests, with the requisite skill set to "get 'er done." The mentor's job is to whip you into shape, while the sponsor's job is to reap the rewards.

The last thing I'll say about the difference between mentors and sponsors has to do with repercussions. People aren't likely to be taken aback by the presence of mentors in your life. If they are, it's because they're jealous. The easiest way to avoid such commotion is by exercising a little discretion. No one needs to know who your mentors are, or what it is you talk about. One of the worst things you can do in Corporate America is "put your business in the streets." You get to choose your mentors, while your mentors get to agree to your terms. And mentors don't mind operating behind the scenes in the course of helping you to land, front and center.

But you don't get to choose sponsors; sponsors get to choose you. Once that happens, it's you who must agree to their terms, which could prove to be a source of great concern for others. Sponsors are nearly impossible to keep under wraps. They have very high profiles, and clear agendas which you are expected to champion. While doing their bidding, you will face opposing forces, one of whom might be your immediate boss. Sponsors, however, assume you have conflict resolution skills good enough to keep their affairs afloat. Unlike mentors, sponsors come with strings attached, which in effect make you their puppet. All that matters is the answer to the question, "What have you done for me, lately?" Absent anything to tout over an extended period in time, you are more or less a dead man, walking.

Monsters are unhappy campers who'd like nothing better than to make your life a living hell. They are not to be confused with assholes, who are content with merely getting in your way. Monsters won't be satisfied until you are literally drummed from the corps. They usually come from the ranks of people who have a bone to pick with you, for reasons either real or imagined. It could be a peer who believes you are standing in his or her way, a boss who thinks you betrayed his or her trust, or a sponsor who's feeling neglected. No matter how hopeless, it's incumbent upon you to look for ways to soothe these savage beasts.

No Guts, No Glory

"To get to something, you must go through something." And so it goes in Corporate America. Scaling the corporate ladder is pretty much the same as running an endless gauntlet. Monsters are, mercifully, of lesser concern, inasmuch as they are relatively few in number. The real threat is posed by worthy adversaries, most of whom are fond of laying booby traps. Their hidden agendas, cloaked in ulterior motives, are designed to catch you off guard. What'll truly blow your mind is the sad realization that even allies may be prone to deceive. Should your good fortune come at their expense, I shudder to think what might happen.

Luckily for me, growing up in the ghetto served as a form of basic training. My formative years were spent running the gauntlet in an area measuring less than ten square miles. It was bordered by the Harlem River to the east, the Hudson River to the west, the Apollo Theater to the south, and Yankee Stadium to the north. Within these boundaries lay a world of wonder, fraught with a curious blend of good and evil. An urban mecca doubled as a killing field, courtesy of bigotry, drugs, and random violence.

The summer fun of 1964 was rudely interrupted by racial riots and the stench of martial law. On February 21, 1965, I was knocking down jump shots in a local park when less than four blocks away, in the Audubon Ballroom, Malcolm X was being knocked down, jumped, shot, and left for dead. Like it or not, I lived in a world that required me to be *en garde* at all times. Danger lurked around every corner, and once I left home, I was totally exposed. Gangbangers, junkies, renegade cops, and robbers were all part of the daily scene. Between flirting with death and chasing ladies, I barely had chance to catch a breath.

My parents sought to keep me on the straight and narrow by behaving as if they were sponsors. There was a code of conduct which they put into effect that was "positively" non-negotiable. Whenever I got busted for disobeying orders, I knew I could kiss my black ass good-bye. Corporal punishment was a staple in the Thomas household, and I got spanked, early and often. Had political correctness been in vogue at that time, my folks would have been thought of as child abusers. From their point of view, sparing the rod was not an option, because a spoiled child in my neighborhood amounted to easy prey. Their brand of tough love enabled me to make wise decisions in the face of life-threatening choices. To further ensure that my act was in order, they converted to Catholicism, bypassed the public school system, and delivered me unto parochial school.

The Benedictine Sisters of St. Mark the Evangelist Elementary School and the Christian Brothers of La Salle Academy High turned out to be mentors of the first and highest order. Their sole purpose in life was to groom me, academically, while providing a moral compass. They insisted that I pursue my ABCs in earnest and live my life by the Word of God. When they were finished with me, I was sharp as a tack, the Lord was my shepherd, and I could walk through the valley of the shadow of death, including Harlem, without fear of any evil. Coming of age in the ghetto, with God as my witness, made scaling the corporate ladder seem more like child's play.

It is neither my intent to convert you to Catholicism nor to ask you to walk a mile in my shoes. Corporate America is a microcosm of the USA, wherein people come from all walks of life. WASPs feel most at home in Corporate America by virtue of being the original architects. Males of the Jewish persuasion have gotten cozy by virtue of their penchant to accumulate wealth. Anyone else who crosses the corporate threshold will discover the welcome mat hard to find. People of color and the fairer sex are often treated like bastard children at the family picnic.

Such harsh reality should come as no surprise when you take American history into account. The Bill of Rights took the rights of minorities and women for granted, rendering them children of a lesser God. Their inalienable rights, as opposed to being proffered, have since been vigorously fought for, tooth and nail. God only knows where the nation's first second-class citizens would be without other constitutional amendments, Supreme Court decisions, and something called affirmative action. Minorities and women are the best living proof of God's will to help those who help themselves.

The indomitable spirit of minorities and women is now holding sway in Corporate America. Glass ceilings are broken by the "unwashed masses" as a matter of routine. But a cold day in hell will follow the twelfth of never before white males give up the ghost. Their fighting spirit, which is second to none, is what sparked the American Revolution. For an encore, they fashioned an Industrial Revolution, parlaying derring-do into capital gains. While many of these gains were ill-gotten, you have to give it up to the sum of their success.

History has shown that the road to success is best traveled by the sly, the slick, and the wicked. And so it goes in Corporate America. Sly is a function of spotting opportunities and knowing when and where to make a move. Slick is a function of making those moves without drawing too much enemy fire. Wicked is a function of making moves that involve collateral damage. Each of these maneuvers is a useful tool in the course of building a rewarding career. Minorities and women have come to be sly and slick by coping with the scourge of inequality. As masters of the universe and most things corporate, white males are good at being wicked.

Whether you are male, female, black, white, or all other, scaling the corporate ladder is a function of making sly, slick, and wicked moves, on behalf of sponsors, aided by mentors. Simply stated, yes, but easier said than done. All moves expose you to certain risks: the risk of making mistakes, the risk of being embarrassed, and worst of all, the risk of failure. Humans have a natural-born aversion toward taking risks, which is systemically reinforced from cradle to grave. Playing it safe seems instinctively wiser than skating on thin ice. But if you're destined to hit pay dirt in Corporate America, you will necessarily learn to ignore these primal instincts. "Nothing ventured, nothing gained" is the clarion call of a good corporate soldier.

I'm through with waxing philosophical on how one ought to behave in Corporate America. Since actions speak louder than words, it's time to tell you how I happened to behave myself. By heeding my words and taking my lead, you too might turn work into something wonderful. So, without further ado, here's an overview of my traipsing up *and* down the corporate ladder.

HELLO, CRUEL WORLD

I remember my first day on the job like it was yesterday, and for the record, yesterday sucked. Gone forever
were the lazy days of summer, the innocence of a slightly
misspent youth, and the succor of collegial surroundings.
The seismic shift from hitting the books hard to working
hard for the money damn near knocked me to my knees.
In more literary terms, "the best of times" morphed into
"the worst of times," thus "scaring the dickens out of
me." Prepared as I might have been to pursue adulthood,
I wasn't quite finished being a kid. Looking back on it now,
I must confess that there was "nothing to fear but fear
itself." Corporate America would serve as my new play-
ground, and God's providence would deliver me unto the
Allstate Insurance Company.

Allstate and I were meant for each other, but we got
off to a rocky start. First, there was the two-week-long
interview process, which can best be described as tor-
ture. I met with no fewer than ten different people, ranging
from human resources personnel to prospective supervisors, managers, and co-workers. While that psychobab-
ble melodrama was inexorably unfolding, complete with
a physical exam and a Rorschach test, Allstate was quietly

performing an exhaustive background check, the likes of which included a police report, credit report, and motor vehicle report. Allstate managed to check me for everything but drugs, which in those days was not the standard practice it has since become. Whew.

I thought that if I could just find a way to survive this rigmarole, the job was in the bag. Not so. Allstate took its sweet time getting to know me and would require me to get to know it. As far as I was concerned, this was overkill. All I cared about was providing for my family without resorting to a life of crime. Allstate was on the verge of making that dream come true, which was good enough for me. But the good folks at Allstate were not about to make me an offer until they had a chance to strut their stuff.

Allstate was a wholly owned subsidiary of Sears, Roebuck & Co., at the time we met in 1972. Legend has it that the CEO, Robert E. Wood, was sold on the idea of starting up a direct-mail automobile insurance company by his neighbor and insurance broker, Carl Odell, while playing bridge during their train commute to and from work. In April 1931, Allstate opened for business. Lessing J. Rosenwald was chairman, Carl Odell was vice president, and twenty people were on the payroll. Four decades later, Allstate had become the crown jewel in Sears' corporate tiara, with more than 30,000 employees and 6,500 insurance agents. It wanted me to know that it was a company on the move, committed to accelerated growth.

Adding to Allstate's corporate panache was its organizational structure. There were twenty-eight regional offices spread throughout the country. Each regional office offered a variety of entry-level positions in one of at least seven different departments. Those departments were known as sales, underwriting, claims, controller, services, human resources, and public affairs. There were four zones, and the best and brightest within each department might eventually be offered a promotion to any one of those offices, or to corporate headquarters, also known as Home Office. Moving between regions, zones, and Home Office would be a necessary part of the deal for those who were committed to professional growth.

The last impression Allstate sought to lay on me was that it was a company flush with cash. Its good fortune came courtesy of parent company Sears, which during the early '70s was "the place where America shopped." While Americans shopped, they couldn't help but notice the gaggle of Allstate Insurance agents nestled beneath escalators in Sears' stores nationwide. This made for a distribution channel that was the envy of an entire industry, given its size, scope, and ability to generate sales. By 1973, Allstate's return to Sears was accounting for nearly 30 percent of its annual earnings.

Allstate's good fortune was best put on display in a short feature film the company produced called *The Allstate Story In Brief.* The film was narrated by none other than Ed Reimers, who preceded Dennis Haysbert as the company's celebrity spokesperson. He spoke in deep, mellow, pear-shaped tones, which, if you didn't know better, sounded like the voice of God. While listening to Ed attest to Allstate's financial prowess, you were treated to a visual tour of the company's commercial real estate holdings. The office buildings looked more like country clubs, which I'm certain was done by design. Each was neatly tucked away beneath the soft suburban underbelly of a major metropolitan city.

The office I sat in while watching the film was known as the Atlanta Region. Located outside the city limits of Atlanta, it sat on several acres of lush, converted farmland in the suburban town of Marietta, Georgia. Looking around, I couldn't help but wonder if the film was doing this place justice. The two-story building had a white marble façade, which glistened by day and glowed at night. Ceiling-to-floor bay windows featured a 360-degree panoramic view of manicured lawns, a small forest, an off-the-street employee parking lot, and a designated picnic area. By the time Allstate's *Story in Brief* was finally told, my eyes were filled with anxious tears of joy.

If I had to go to work for the rest of my life, this seemed like a pretty good place to start. Unfortunately, Allstate continued to play it cool, which began to get on my nerves. They wanted more time to consider my application, but promised to call me within a few days to inform me of their final decision. Much to my relief, I was called the next day and from there my journey took flight.

I reported for duty on October 3, 1972, as if I had won a Powerball lottery. What a wonderful feeling it was to literally be "In Good Hands with Allstate"! I could hardly wait for the workday to end, so I could rush to the nearest Sears store and buy some automobile insurance. I proudly introduced myself to the Allstate agent stationed beneath the escalator as a newly hired underwriter trainee. At first he flinched, for reasons I'll explain later. Then he gently smiled, welcomed me aboard, and started filling out the application.

Upon completing the application, the agent's expression turned grim. He reluctantly informed me that, due to certain underwriting guidelines, he would be unable to submit my application. Apparently, I was good enough to hire, but not good enough to insure. Walking out of the store with my tail between my legs, I wondered, "What manner of bullshit is this?!" In order to appreciate the cruel irony, you need to understand how insurance works.

How Insurance Works

Insurance companies are in the business of making money with your money. You give it to them, and they promise to give it back to you one day, someday, or maybe not. Simple as that. I exaggerate a bit, which isn't fair. Here's a better sense of how they operate.

An insurance company promises to reimburse you in the event of an insured loss. The losses you need protection from will determine the type of policy you purchase. There are policies to accommodate a wide range of needs. You can buy insurance for your business, life, health, home, automobile, apartment, condominium, boat, motor home, motorcycle, what have you. The more stuff you have, the more stuff they have to sell you, all of which keeps insurance companies rolling in your dough.

In exchange for its promise, you agree to pay the company annual premiums based in part on the law of large numbers. The law of large numbers can be readily expressed as follows: "The observed frequency of an event more nearly approaches the underlying probability of the population as the number of trials approaches infinity." Huh? Here's another way to look at it.

It's easy to predict how often an insured loss will occur once an insured group gets exponentially larger. That number is called *average frequency*. Once a company can safely predict how often an insured loss will occur, it then seeks to determine the average cost of each event. By dividing annual losses by frequency of events, you arrive at what's known as *average severity*.

For this arrangement to work smoothly, companies must adhere to the basic principles of insurance. Among other things, these principles require a large number of homogeneous exposures and sufficient capital to pay for expected losses. Sufficient capital is commonly referred to as *reserves,* and the business model works as follows: the company charges you a premium and invests that money over a period in time. The premiums it collects and the investment income it derives should amount to at least 10 percent more than it will ever pay out in claims, given the frequency and severity of losses. That excess amount is known as *profit.* When a company lies in ruins because it ignores the basic principles of insurance, it's known as **AIG**.

None of this explains why Allstate would deny me auto insurance, and I apologize for that. It's just that I thought it was important to describe how insurance companies operate in general before getting into the specifics of Allstate's business model. Though best known in the '70s for providing auto insurance, Allstate offered a wide range of personal lines, along with property and casualty products. Personal lines refer to insurance sold to an individual or family as opposed to a business. Property and casualty refers to automobile, homeowners, boaters, renters, etc. Allstate's portfolio included life insurance and commercial insurance, as well. Each of these products was offered through an exclusive, captive-agent network. Unique for its time, Allstate agents were the only people licensed to sell products on behalf of Allstate Insurance.

Regions were expected to exploit the power of this distribution channel in conjunction with other business units. Each of these units, housed in departments, was headed by a regional manager. Here's how the pieces fit together.

Allstate fancied itself a sales organization when I was entering the fold. What that meant was that Allstate would never be satisfied until it was the largest domestic personal lines insurer. The only thing standing in its way was State Farm Insurance. The Home Office would be responsible for corporate governance, investing, product development, pricing, and advertising. The zones would be responsible for keeping tabs on the regions. And the regions would be responsible for using their "*Good Hands*" to beat their "*Good Neighbors*" down.

The sales department was by far the first among equals within the regional group of seven. All of those managers drove company cars, lived in big houses, and came and went as they pleased. Only agents could have it better than they. Agents were directly responsible for the company's top-line growth. In return for their efforts, they were richly rewarded in relation to their written premiums. New business sales netted 15 percent, while renewals netted 3–5 percent. The highest-paid agents, on average, were knocking down six-figure incomes, easily.

Newly hired agents were placed beneath escalators and left there until they proved proficient at writing and retaining business. Once they established a sizeable book of business, they were ushered into a cushy neighborhood sales office. The highest-producing agents in any given year were treated to trips around the world, all expenses paid. Agents were the most privileged of regional employees, and everybody knew it. The only ones empowered to slightly rain on an agent's parade were known as underwriters. And that explains why the agent flinched when I introduced myself.

To have some agents tell it, underwriters were nothing more than weasely, little, green-eyed monsters, jealous of an agent's lot in life and fond of eating their young. As far as some underwriters were concerned, agents were nothing more than greedy, little, money-grubbing bastards who would sell insurance to the living dead for the sake of their own selfish interests. Both points of view were pretty much bogus, but I can see how they came to be.

Every application written by an agent was subject to an underwriter's review. This review was used to determine whether the premium being charged was enough to cover the risk. After the review, a decision was made to either accept or reject the application. If the risk was accepted, the agent got paid. If it wasn't, the agent got nada. Less than 10 percent of all applications were rejected because agents were equipped with underwriting guidelines. As long as agents followed these guidelines, their business was usually put on the books.

There were underwriting guidelines for every line of insurance. In the case of auto insurance, here's what the guidelines stated: zero accidents or moving violations in the past three years, and no more than one of either in the past five years; conservative cars; prior insurance in force with another company; and no SMT. SMT was the acronym for "special marketing territory." Special marketing territories were designated "no write zones," and this practice was known as "redlining." I was living in a redlined area at the time. And now you know why the agent told me that he couldn't submit my application.

The practice of redlining is no longer legal, but underwriting lives on. In a sales organization obsessed with top-line growth, it was left to underwriting and others to protect the bottom line. Their guidelines controlled average frequency, but what about average severity, you might ask.

The answer to your question is the claims department. As comrades in arms, they often joked that "agents wrote business that you guys accepted, and now we're paying for your mistakes!" Their job was to settle claims, in accordance with policy terms, for the least amount of money. How's that for a tacky chore? Their frontline employees were called adjusters. As a group, they easily came to earn my respect and sympathy. What a bitch it must have been serving two masters with diametrically opposed needs. Adjusters had superiors looking over one shoulder while claimants were crying on the other. It took the cunning of Sherlock Holmes and the compassion of Mother Teresa to keep everybody happy.

Those in the controllers department didn't give a damn about happy. Why else would they call themselves that? The name itself inspired contempt, as did the very nature of their work. They spent their days poring over mechanized financial reports in desperate search of adverse trends in sales, underwriting, and claims. And as soon as they found some dirt, they'd go running off to the regional manager's office to share the sinister findings. The best that can be said for people in the controllers department was that they usually numbered fewer than five.

The services department was a friend to one and all. These people were in charge of administrative stuff vital to keeping our doors open for business. They would eventually change their name to *operations* in order to more accurately reflect their mission. The human resources department was even more beloved, because it administered employee benefits. Last, and probably least, was the public affairs department. There were only two people in public affairs: the department manager and his secretary. No one knew for sure what they did.

These were the members of my new extended family. As with any large clan, we had our small differences. Sales fought with underwriting; underwriting fought with services; zones fought regions; and everybody fought Home Office. But the common cause that brought us all together was the quest to be number one.

GETTING DOWN TO BUSINESS

People lie and accidents happen. That's why the world needs underwriters. Let me explain. An insurance company charges premiums based on a given risk. These premiums are established by actuarial science, which applies mathematical and statistical methods. If an actuary tells you that it will take X amount of dollars to cover a risk and generate a modest profit, you can take that to the bank. Actuaries know what they're talking about. Their actuarial tables can effectively predict the date and time when people will die! That's how they establish life insurance premiums.

Tables are also used to promulgate property and casualty premiums. Take auto insurance, for example. Every vehicle on the road poses a certain risk based on its age, make, and model. The degree of risk is further influenced by the person behind the wheel. On one extreme, you have the newly licensed, teen-aged driver. On the other, you have the kindly, little old man. Now throw into the mix a wide variety of other risk factors, such as driving record, prior insurance history, use of car (business, to and from work, or pleasure), annual miles driven (7,500 or fewer), principally garaged (urban, suburban, or rural), and what you end up with is an exposure for which there can only be one fair price.

If new business apps were taken at face value, it wouldn't take long before Allstate went bust. It was the underwriter's job to search for absolute truth related to premium versus exposure. We ordered motor vehicle reports on all known drivers, looking for undisclosed activity. In certain cases, we went so far as to look for undisclosed drivers. How would you handle an app for a married couple, between the ages of forty-five and fifty, with four cars in the household, two of which were fit for teens, and no young drivers listed? Damn right, you'd order an inspection! Six out of ten new business applications typically contained false, incomplete, or misleading information, which resulted in either higher premium charges or outright rejection.

Underwriters were obliged to examine our "in force" book of business, as well. The point of this review was to identify customers with poor loss experience. Distinctions were made between "fault" and "non-fault" losses. Contributory negligence was also taken into account. But once it was determined that a customer no longer qualified as a "good driver," he or she was cut from the herd of other good drivers in order to preserve "good-driver rates." Approximately 3–5 percent of our book would be "non-renewed," and offered a new policy at a substantially higher rate. Customers with DUI (driving under the influence) losses were non-renewed with extreme prejudice.

Regardless of cause, no one likes to be rejected, cancelled, or non-renewed. In the agents' case, it affects their income. In the customers' case, it affects their sense of pride. Given the naughty nature of their work, underwriters were well served to become skilled negotiators and artful communicators. A lot of their time was spent on the phone with customers or in meetings with agents, defending the propriety of their decisions. Absent the ability to leave their audience with reasonable explanations and/or options to choose from, it's the underwriters' jobs that likely would be terminated. It took two years to develop my multi-line underwriting chops. This proved to be the easiest part of my job. Witness the fact that after only one week on the job, I was able to approve my own auto application.

The hardest part of my job was conforming to the unwritten rules of proper business conduct. In many respects, I behaved like a silly little kid instead of sober-minded corporate soldier. It was not at all uncommon for me to walk around the region, slapping people "high fives" for no apparent reason. Nor was it uncommon for me to flirt with the ladies, both young and old, while they were working at their desks. The most grievous crime I was often guilty of was arriving late for work. On those rare occasions when I made it in on time, my co-workers would greet me with a standing ovation. I was in desperate need of a mentor's help to save me from myself.

My very first mentor was an underwriter by the name of Mike Jett. He, too, had joined Allstate fresh out of college, three years prior to my arrival. Mike was no stranger to my shenanigans. He was something of a free spirit himself. But he quickly learned from the error of his ways and saw fit to teach me a thing or two. He noted that my social butterfly, Johnny-come-lately style was making it difficult if not impossible for people to take me seriously. Since the art of underwriting was no laughing matter, it was critically important for us underwriters to act like professionals. He further noted that my boyish charm and outgoing personality would best serve me during morning, lunch, and late afternoon breaks.

Soon after getting the hang of proper business conduct, I encountered my very first sponsor. His name was Bill Gilstrap. He was not only the underwriting department manager but also something of an Allstate legend. Bill had left a sleepy backwoods town in Georgia, lured by the bright city lights of Atlanta. Upon his arrival, he would eventually land a job in the Atlanta region's mailroom. Through many years of distinguished service, Bill would subsequently find himself in charge of underwriting.

This was quite a feat for a country bumpkin who, unlike his fellow department managers, supposedly earned his stripes without a college degree or a need to relocate. The only manager commanding more respect than Bill was the regional manager, W. Garland Loftis, to whom they all reported. The majority of Bill's time was spent in his office, usually behind closed doors. If he wasn't huddled with his management staff, I assumed he was on the phone with Garland. On those rare occasions when he mingled with his troops, I found myself marveling at the cut of his jib.

I had no reason to suspect that Bill was admiring the cut of my jib. Turns out, I was wrong. Unbeknownst to me, Bill thought I might be management material. Turns out, he was right. Before jumping to any false conclusions, Bill took it upon himself to get to know me better. After getting me comfortable in his presence, Bill invited me to his office, closed the door, and asked me about my long-term goals. I told him that if I could ever bring home thirty thousand dollars a year, I'd die a happy man. He quickly countered that I could one day sit in his chair, at which time I simply laughed in his face.

Bill was hardly joking as he ordered me to compose myself. Then he started talking in earnest terms about something called affirmative action. It seemed the company was under pressure from the federal government to advance the promotion of qualified minorities and women. That alone should have been reason enough for me to believe that equal opportunities abounded. But it was Bill's choosing to believe in me as a person that made all the difference in the world.

Affirmative action may well have been just a passing fancy, but self-reliance was everlasting. That was Bill's position, and he admonished me to take the same. In effect, he was challenging me to play the corporate game to the best of my abilities and let the chips fall where they may. Playing the corporate game would require me to be both an individual star and a team player. If my personal best turned out to be crucial to the team's overall success, then with or without affirmative action, I could anticipate a very bright future.

Before taking Bill's advice to heart, I had to put his words into a working context. How could a novice underwriter like me affect the fortunes of Allstate? The answer was under my nose. The extent to which my personal best made the underwriting department look good was the extent to which I could fulfill Bill's prophecy. The best place to start would be within my unit.

The underwriting department in the Atlanta region consisted of four units. There were two underwriter units assigned to states within our jurisdiction, namely Georgia and Alabama. The other two units within the department were known as examiners and clerks. Collectively, we were responsible for processing new and renewal business written between the two states.

In those days, Allstate was a virtual paper mill, and the workload was delivered by truckloads. Clerks were responsible for opening the mail, placing it in files, and preparing them for review. Examiners would then process run-of-the-mill files not worthy of any special attention.

Everything else was up for underwriter grabs, and that was usually more than a handful.

Because Allstate was growing by leaps and bounds, the overflow of business was a constant challenge. Nothing was more harmful to employee morale than being deluged by a sea of files. The best-case scenario for our department was to "zero out" every day. Zeroing out meant that daily receipts were fully processed by the end of the day. The worst-case scenario was being overwhelmed by something called "carryover."

Carryover was the term for unprocessed business, something anathema within the region. When carryover got heavy, bad things happened. Customers worried about being accepted, sales worried about meeting weekly goals, and agents worried about their commission checks. A few days of carryover was no big deal. A week's worth was nettlesome. Anything more was cause for great concern because all management hell would break loose.

The summer of 1975 proffered my first chance to rise and shine. The department's workload was getting out of hand, considering the three weeks' worth of carryover, and counting. And bad attitudes were beginning to develop in what was otherwise a very *Brady Bunch* office. Underwriters would complain about being understaffed. Managers would complain about lollygagging. There was something to be said for both arguments, but this was clearly a call for action.

A Fourth of July weekend was all the time I needed to turn the situation from grim to great. Over those three days, I managed to process every single file that sat in our department. My co-workers returned on Monday, July 7, pleasantly surprised to find nothing to do. Managers were also happy little campers, but none more so than Bill. No one had to tell him who the rainmaker was. Nor did anyone have to tell Bill who was deserving of a promotion.

A lot has changed since I started my career at Allstate more than thirty years ago. Paper files are a thing of the past, and some people are working from home. For those of you who are still working in an office, there's something to be taken from my experience. The first thing you need to recognize is that "all work is a process." Part of being proficient in your job is knowing how it links to others. This not only applies to the jobs within your unit/department, but to the ones outside it as well. Lacking an understanding of how the pieces fit together means that your brain can never be picked for any bright ideas on how to make the process flow better.

Another thing I would encourage you to do is take responsibility for problem solving. Such an effort should be applied to problems you cause, as well as those affecting your department. Learning to take ownership for problem solving is the first step toward establishing yourself as management material. Problem solving usually requires teamwork, and there's nothing stopping you from putting an informal team together. This is all the more reason for knowing how the pieces fit together. How else would you know whom to draft, or why?

The last thing I would suggest for now is that you get to know the big boss. By big boss, I'm referring to your department head, which most likely is not your immediate supervisor. Your objective here is to formally introduce yourself, especially if you've never met. Let him or her know that you appreciate this golden opportunity and look forward to serving him or her well. Don't look now, but each of these maneuvers is a discreet form of kissing ass.

For what it's worth, what I'm trying to do is help establish you as a force to be reckoned with. Any old body can sit in an office building, occupy space, do a decent job, and go home. That's what you'd call a deadbeat. On the opposite end of the worker-bee spectrum is what you'd call a go-getter. Webster's defines a go-getter as "*an aggressively enterprising person.*" What that translates to in the corporate world is a take-charge kind of guy or gal who's not afraid to push the boundaries of convention on behalf of positive change.

This bold and daring approach, combined with a good feel for people, a fearless attitude, and a-cut-above-average skills, is exactly what allowed me to ease my way out of the rank and file into management. Why couldn't it be the same for you? Management is defined as the "*judicious use of means to accomplish an end.*" Notice there was no mention of insurance. Management skills can be applied equally to any line of work you choose.

MOVING UP TO LOWER MANAGEMENT

The ongoing development of my technical skills afforded me an opportunity to manage people. I could study insurance contracts without lapsing into a coma or suffering damage to the brain. I could reject, cancel, and non-renew with my left hand, while agents quietly ate from my right. None of these adaptive skills was proof positive that I could entreat people to follow my lead. So underwriting chieftains hedged their bets by placing me in a position where I could do the least amount of damage.

I began the development of my management skills by lording it over the clerical unit. There were twelve clerks in all, whose demographic makeup included single parents, empty nesters, the happily married, the recently divorced, a newlywed, a widow, and a part-time college student. They ranged in age from nineteen to fifty-nine. And by the way, did I happen to mention that the unit was 100 percent female? Talk about a bitches brew!

Now, don't get me wrong; this was a fine group of ladies. But as individuals, they needed to be handled with kid gloves. They were the lowest-paid employees in a high-powered department, earning barely more than minimum wage. They worked on behalf of some underwriters who hardly knew they existed. The final indignation was working for a steady stream of supervisors who had never supervised before. At best, we were thought of as interlopers who would soon be moving on, no matter what.

I could easily relate to their sense of getting short shrift in light of the time I spent in the hood. My natural instinct was to care for them as people first and then as employees. At the start of each day, I would sit on the edge of every clerk's desk and chat with her about anything and everything except work. We talked about their families, their favorite TV shows, what they had for dinner, or their favorite movie stars. Whatever they wanted to share with me was what I wanted to know.

They came to look forward to these daily encounters, and, in many respects, it was the highlight of my day. In the time it took to win each other's hearts and minds, we transformed ourselves from a ragtag bunch of lesser lights into the fittest unit in the department. There was nothing I couldn't ask these ladies to do for me in the name of taking care of our business. In return, they knew they could count on me to look out for their very best interests.

Trying to win the hearts and minds of people within my charge became a management imperative. It gave me a chance to earn an employee's trust, which is the currency of leadership. The same drill I used in the clerical unit proved invaluable throughout my career. Once it was established that I had a knack for rallying troops, it was high time to develop other skills.

Moving through lower management would require me to learn how to swim with baby sharks. There was a friendly competition brewing between myself and three other supervisors. Each of us had designs on the division manager's position, which was second in command to Bill. Looking at the field objectively, I felt like the odds-on favorite. And if by chance I didn't win, I would have considered the race fair and square.

The stiffest competition I faced in the department was from my best friend, Tom Falkenbach. Tom and I started as underwriter trainees less than two months apart. He was a graduate of Florida State whom I took a shine to from the first day we met. He was single, good-looking, and drove a hot car, a silver Porsche Carrera, as I recall. More importantly, like me, Tom was a sports junky who enjoyed playing as much as watching. Tom would be my brother from another mother to the extent such things exist.

The only other supervisor with a decent shot at the title was a young lady named Linda Gibson. Linda was a transplant from our Ohio regional office by way of her husband's transfer with another company. Linda had more management experience than Tom and I had, combined. Yet I didn't consider her much of a threat as long as she was tethered to her spouse's career. I would rue the day that I jumped to such a hasty conclusion.

The incumbent division manager whose job we coveted was none other than Mike Jett, my original Allstate mentor. Mike and I had maintained a close working relationship over the course of my fledgling career. In fact, I often teased him with some conviction about being the wind beneath his wings. That was all the more reason to feel good about my chances of replacing him one day. Before that day dawned, I had to overcome an obstacle that threatened to seriously break my stride.

I can still see the sober look on Mike's face as he approached my desk and asked me to join him in his office. As we walked in dead silence back to Mike's office, I could sense that this was going to be a dreadful meeting for both of us. I took a seat; Mike closed the door and wasted no time rendering bad news. Someone in the department had told Bill Gilstrap that I was showing up for work with alcohol on my breath! Given the nature of our relationship, he shared with me in confidence that the person was none other than Linda Gibson. *What a bitch!*

A disconsolate Bill was waiting for me in his office. How could I possibly defend myself against such a hideous charge? Mike's advice was to tell the truth, and then he hastened me to be on my way. I found Bill sitting uncomfortably behind his desk. He motioned me to enter and close the door. He knew Mike had apprised me of the controversy. Now it was time for me to tell my side of the story. I took a deep breath, looked Bill squarely in the eye, and told him, "*I occasionally drink before coming to work in order to mask the smell of marijuana.*"

Bill might have swallowed his corncob pipe were it not for the brute force of his belly laugh. Tears began streaming down his face, which were either from anger or comic relief. In the time it took for Bill to pull himself together, I assured him that this was all one great big misunderstanding. Perhaps it was cough syrup Linda had smelled; I had been nursing a cold for nearly a month, to which each of my co-workers could attest. Whatever the case, I was completely innocent, and of that he could be certain.

The incident passed without further comment. My reason for bringing it up is twofold. Keeping your wits about you while under attack is an effective management gambit. A sharp sense of humor can just as easily diffuse a tense situation as getting all hot and bothered or defensive. Something else you should never do is to take your competitors for granted.

In the early spring of 1976, I was once again summoned to Bill's office. This time we were meeting under far better circumstances than we had four months prior. Bill was grinning like the Cheshire cat and I couldn't imagine why.

He took guilty pleasure in allowing me to twist in the wind before letting me in on his little secret. I was being promoted to the position of underwriting division manager in our Dallas, Texas, regional office, effective April 1.

I didn't know whether to blink or go blind. In either case, I was speechless. In a show of affection that was rare for Bill, he warmly embraced me, told me how proud he was of me, and suggested that this was only the beginning. I, in turn, thanked him from the bottom of my heart and promised to stay in touch. The very next thing I thought to do was share the good news with Linda.

I had somewhat mixed emotions about leaving my friends and colleagues behind. It's also fair to say that my wife wasn't entirely pleased with the idea of having to quit her job, take our daughter out of school, and move lock, stock, and barrel more than halfway across the country. Such was the price of success. After settling into our new location, we agreed to make the most of a "glad" situation. She would become a stay at home mom, and I would bring home more bacon.

I took to my new assignment with vim, vigor, and pep. The first thing I did was seek an audience with the regional manager, a gentleman by the name of Bryant Moore. Bryant was a favorite son of Texas, much like Bill Gilstrap was in Georgia. Unlike Bill, Bryant had started his career as an Allstate agent, moved up through the ranks of sales management, done a stint in the Home Office, and returned to the Dallas region as a conquering hero. Agents were on a first-name basis with Bryant, and he wouldn't have it any other way. Most everyone else called him sir.

George Cobb was the underwriting department manager to whom I now reported. He was nothing like Bill, in that he was a bundle of nervous energy who spoke in spurts and was easily distracted. But George knew a lot about the business of insurance, especially underwriting. When I could calm him down for more than five minutes, he was a source of great insight and wisdom.

The Dallas region was nearly twice the size of Atlanta in terms of its customer base, employee count, and agents. George would need two division managers to help him carry the load. Earl Heiderhoff handled new business receipts, while I took care of renewals. Under normal business conditions, mine should have been an easy task. Due to forces beyond my control, it turned out to be anything but.

Technology was being imposed on me in ways that were foreign to my experience. The only way I knew how to process renewal business was to manually review files, one by one. This was a labor-intensive process that was putting a strain on both employees and expenses. A more efficient way of doing business was desperately needed. The company installed an automated program called LEW, which stood for "loss early warning." Thick files were being replaced with thin sheets of paper from which underwriters were to make their decisions.

LEW represented a scale of change that was capable of completely blowing one's mind. Underwriters, by design, are creatures of intense habit who are most comfortable when stuck in procedural mud. It was up to me, the new kid on the block, to convince the region's oldest and most experienced underwriters that good decisions could be made without the benefit of big, fat files. It was also my job to troubleshoot technical glitches that necessarily accompany the introduction of brand-new systems. How lucky could one guy get?

The first thing I had to do was convince myself that such a drastic change wouldn't destroy the bottom line. I took a random sample of one hundred LEW referrals and used the "new and improved" information to reach decisions as to renew or non-renew. Then I snuck into the basement where the files were being stored and retrieved the ones I had reviewed by way of LEW. There were only two decisions that would have resulted in a different outcome, and in both of those cases I would have kept the business on the books. LEW was working like a charm.

I shared the results of my experiment with the most highly regarded underwriter in the division. Then I invited him to conduct his own experiment. Thank God his results were much the same. Together, we assured the rest of the division that it was safe to get on board with LEW. With that mind-set change behind me, I could concentrate on systems issues. Three months into the conversion, we were singing the praises of LEW. Go figure.

Just when I thought I could kick back, relax, and enjoy my first office, all manner of a far more frightening hell broke loose. Agents had gotten wind of LEW and now they were on the warpath. When agents were unhappy, Bryant Moore was unhappy. When Bryant Moore was unhappy, look out. It was only a matter of time before he would be knocking on my office door, probably using George's head.

Agents were telling Bryant that my underwriters were using LEW as an excuse to non-renew higher volumes of business. I countered that claim by sharing with Bryant a series of weekly LEW reports, which showed that non-renewals were on par with prior years. Unfortunately, Bryant wasn't into this form of empirical data. What he wanted was a new procedure. Bryant would personally review every LEW decision before sending each off to be processed.

Now, Bryant had every right to second-guess our decisions, and I admired his gung-ho spirit. What bothered me was the fact that Bryant was a piss-poor underwriter, and would undo good decisions based on misguided loyalties.

Every morning I would receive five or six LEW decisions that Bryant ordered reversed, not because it was good business, but because he was doing favors. It was driving me out of my mind.

George could sense my mounting frustration and waited for an opening to set me straight. He reminded me of something I had obviously forgotten: Allstate was a sales organization. For every renewal Bryant saved for an agent, he could count on that same agent to produce higher volumes of new business. George further explained that the company was in the midst of what he called a *growth cycle*, but in time the pendulum would swing. And when it did, the emphasis would switch from revenue growth to bottom-line profits, prompting Bryant to back off and let underwriting do its thing.

After carefully considering what George had to say, I started to get the big picture. Bryant was simply doing what came naturally, and it would be wise of me to go along to get along. Put another way, George was suggesting that I think about what Bryant was doing as being "fantastic" as opposed to "bullshit." As soon as I altered my frame of reference, everything was copacetic. This attitude adjustment was quickly followed by a chance encounter with a character who would favorably rock my world for many years to come.

That someone was a guy by the name of Larry Davies. Larry was the underwriting department manager in the Kansas City regional office. What brought us together was a territorial realignment that affected our respective regions. The Dallas region would merge with the Houston region to become the Texas region. Before doing so, we needed to cede jurisdiction for the state of Oklahoma to the Kansas City region. Larry was in town to be briefed on matters pertaining to the implications of this trade.

George appointed me official liaison between Larry and the newly formed Texas region. Unofficially, I was Larry's gopher, as in "go for this, go for that." Protocol dictated that I pre-register Larry in a swank hotel and await his arrival in the lobby. At a predetermined time, Larry was told to look for a young black man, nattily attired, wearing a Good Hands lapel pin. I spotted him before he spotted me, thanks to some karmic connection. After a firm handshake and a friendly "how do you do," it was up to Larry to determine our next move.

Since it was five o'clock in the afternoon, his options were unlimited. What I suspected was that Larry would want to talk shop. What I feared was his wanting us to go our separate ways. Much to my pleasant surprise, Larry wanted neither. What he suggested, instead, was adjourning to the hotel rooftop bar. There, we would have a chance to get to know each other over a couple of frosty libations. To say that we hit it off famously would be the understatement of a lifetime.

Larry was a hardscrabble street kid from Philadelphia by way of Ketchikan, Alaska. He cursed like a sailor, drank like a fish, and had a watchful eye for pretty ladies. That alone was good enough to impress the hell out of me. What made him absolutely irresistible was the measure of his success.

Larry had begun his career as an underwriter trainee in the Valley Forge region, circa 1968. In the eight years that followed, Larry was promoted on five different occasions: eastern zone underwriter, division manager in the Milwaukee region, division manager in the Michigan region, department manager in the Indianapolis region, and department manager in the Kansas City region. This sort of ladder climbing was unheard of at Allstate, especially in underwriting.

I was obviously in the presence of a wunderkind, but he was also a down-to-earth, regular guy. After several hours of easy banter, I found myself thinking, *Mike wants to be like Larry.* He was smart as a whip, upwardly mobile, and apparently well connected. I also got the impression from listening to him talk that being good at your job was not nearly good enough. If I were ever going to enjoy Larry's success, I would have to keep in mind the immortal words of Oliver Cromwell, who said, "He who stops being better, stops being good."

After an uneventful meeting early the next morning, I drove Larry back to the airport and bid him a fond adieu. Little did I know I'd be working for him in less than twenty-four months. Meanwhile, I would focus my energies on matching his impressive track record. The first anniversary of my days as a division manager was rapidly approaching when rumors started circulating about a potential move to Home Office. No one was more surprised than I.

I was just getting settled in my new position as division manager, learning things day by day. What made these rumors all the more peculiar was that if they were true, my next promotion, after spending a year in Home Office, would be to the position of department manager. That was the natural order of progression based on a time-honored, ironclad precedent. As much as I wanted to match Larry's record, I didn't want to do it "on the fly."

As the rumors grew more intense, I grew more suspicious. There was a black man by the name Ed Connors currently working in Home Office underwriting. The rumor mill had it that he was moving out under less than happy circumstances, and I would be the one to take his place. If this was the company's idea of supporting affirmative action, I wanted nothing to do with it. I took my concerns to George, and he promised to check things out.

Shortly thereafter, George confirmed that Home Office underwriting was seriously considering bringing me on board. Furthermore, I should expect to be paid a visit by Bill Morris, who was a director in Home Office underwriting. Bill flew into Dallas, took me to lunch, and made me a tentative offer. I shared with Bill the nature of my concerns, which included a laundry list of items. First and foremost, I didn't like the idea of being swapped with another minority for the sake of maintaining an affirmative-action quota.

Moreover, I was just beginning to get the hang of being a division manager. My sense was that I was still growing in the job, not to mention learning a lot from George. If those weren't good enough reasons for Bill to consider someone else, I asked him to consider my family. They were finally getting settled in our new home. My wife was happy in her adopted role and could shop around town without getting hopelessly lost. My four-year-old daughter was happy with her new playmates and no longer crying herself to sleep.

The last thing I wanted to do was sound like an ingrate. I assured Bill that I was flattered by his attention and more than willing to accept his offer if he was certain that I was the right man for the job. The right man for the job was to be defined as someone who would work for a year in Home Office and be ready for promotion to the position of department manager. Anything short of that would be unacceptable.

While I was busy hyperventilating, Bill was calmly chewing his food. Sensing when I was finished making my case, he laid down his knife and fork, wiped his mouth with his sleeve, and responded to my ranting. (Never trust anyone who wipes his mouth with his sleeve!) Bill wanted me to believe, in no uncertain terms, that I was "the only man for the job." There's no such thing as "the only man for the job," but who was I to argue with Bill? He went on to say that my head would be "split open and filled with knowledge," rendering me worthy of becoming a department manager. Sadly for me and my family, Bill was full of shit.

Effective April 1, 1977, I was promoted to Home Office underwriting as a field review manager. The job primarily entailed flying around the country participating in audits. These audits were a corporate staple that involved a matrix of underwriting personnel. There's no way to grasp the inner workings of these audits without a closer look at organizational design. I beseech you, in advance, to bear with me.

Home Office consisted of two component parts. One part managed *internal affairs,* while the other managed *external affairs.* Internal affairs had mostly to do with matters of corporate governance. Departments belonging to internal affairs included Law and Regulation, Compliance, Pricing, Systems, Investments, and Corporate Relations, just to name a few. Essentially, these functions operated behind the scenes, seldom making contact with the public.

Home Office departments in external affairs were a mirror image of what was found in regions; that is to say, sales, underwriting, claims, and so on. Each of these departments was headed by a vice president who had a staff, including assistant vice presidents, directors, and an assortment of mid-level managers, i.e., field-review managers. These were the people who were responsible for making certain that regional counterparts were doing what they were told to do. If they weren't, it was the job of Home Office external affairs to recommend corrective action.

There was another layer of management hierarchy meant to keep a careful eye on the regions. That layer was contained in the four zone offices I referred to long ago. For the sake of decentralization, zone offices were placed outside Home Office, working in tandem with external affairs. Cleverly named after points on a compass, there was the Eastern zone, the Western zone, the Midwest zone, and the Southern zone.

A zone vice president headed each of the four zones. The way one got to be a zone vice president was by having success as a regional manager in a minimum of two regions. They too had a staff that mirrored the region's. There was a zone sales manager, zone underwriting manager, zone claims manager, etc. The way one got to be a zone department manager was by having success as a department manager in a minimum of two regions. Each of the zone department managers had an able-bodied assistant, i.e., zone underwriter. The way one got to be an able-bodied assistant was by having success as a supervisor in one region.

The twenty-eight regional offices were evenly split between the four zone offices on the basis of their geography. Four sets of seven regional managers reported directly to their respective zone vice president. You now know more than you ever cared to know about Allstate's management structure. You also know what you need to know to keep up with my continuing adventures. Let's get back to the business at hand.

Zone vice presidents had the authority to call for field reviews. They would target regions that were underperforming in the areas of revenue growth, bottom-line profits, and expense control. The usual suspects within the region would be the sales, underwriting, and claims departments. When an underwriting department review was called for in any one of the twenty-eight regions, that's when I sprang into action.

I represented Home Office underwriting within an ad hoc committee of other underwriting personnel. Depending on the region under siege, this group consisted of the zone underwriter, supervisors, and division managers in the affiliate zone. This group of five or six people would alight upon the region to begin an audit that lasted from Monday morning through Thursday evening. The audit was designed to look for flaws in the underwriting process that might account for subpar results. Shame on us if we came up empty-handed.

On Thursday evening, we were joined by my boss, Bill Morris, and the affiliate zone-underwriting manager. Over a sumptuous meal and copious drinks, we would share our findings with the overlords and prepare our final report. On Friday morning, the report was covered, sometimes in painful detail. Our audience included the regional manager, the underwriting department manager, and his entire staff. With our dirty work done, we would return to our respective offices, acting as if nothing had happened.

When I wasn't busy digging up dirt, I was hosting something called PLUS. It too was a weeklong exercise, but with a decidedly different tone. PLUS was an acronym that stood for "personal lines underwriting seminar." It was the means by which Home Office underwriting introduced corporate headquarters to first-year underwriters. "Baby underwriters" were brought in from around the country, ensconced in a nearby Holiday Inn, and allowed five days to "mix it up" with Home Office luminaries.

It was my job to identify the highest-ranking officials who could spare an hour of their time to spend with the underwriters. The underwriting vice president would always be on hand, along with his entire staff. More often than not, the chairman of the board would take time from his busy schedule to address the newbies, as well. When the chairman found time to make an appearance, I could count on honchos to turn out in droves. By the time we sent the underwriters packing, they had plenty to talk about when they got home.

None of my assignments was keeping Bill's promise to "fill my head full of knowledge." After eight months on the job, rather than moaning and groaning, I asked Bill if he thought I was holding up my end of the bargain. He assured me that I was "doing a great job," and things were "going according to plan." Three months later, I got a call from a secretary in human resources, which would shed a blinding light on Bill's deception.

I knew this young lady as a result of going to lunch with my secretary several times a month. I would sit with her colleagues and engage in casual conversation as if I were one of their crew. (You'd be surprised at what you might learn while having lunch with a bunch of secretaries!) The purpose of her call was to be one of the first to congratulate me on my soon-to-be-announced promotion.

I had no idea what she was talking about but acted as if I did. When she told me that I would enjoy working for Art Ivey in the Charlotte region, I nearly lost control of my bodily functions. Art Ivey was the underwriting department manager in Charlotte, which meant that I would be working as his division manager. Bill Morris would have known about this move well in advance; in fact, he was probably pulling strings.

One of the worst positions you can find yourself in is working for someone you can't trust. In the case of Bill, I couldn't trust him as far as I could throw him, with a broken arm and two bum knees. It was never Bill's intention to send me out as a department manager. Why that was, I'll never know. My first inclination was to storm Bill's office and commence kicking his ass. That only would have made matters worse. Before returning to the field as a division manager, I had to at least give him a piece of my troubled mind.

I waited for a Friday prior to a Monday when I would be out of town on business. That way, the two of us would have time to reflect on what was said before facing each other again. The first shot I fired across Bill's bow was letting him know that I knew about Charlotte. From the pained expression on his face, you would have thought I had kicked him in the nuts! After Bill hemmed and hawed for what seemed like an hour, I politely interrupted him to get on with what I had to say.

I told Bill that I considered him less than a man, let alone a manager, for having led me astray. He had every opportunity to level with me "from Jump Street," but chose to pull the wool over my eyes. I asked Bill what had inspired him to do as much, and he started hemming and hawing again. Since Bill was incapable of responding coherently, I decided to end the madness by leaving him with one last thought.

Larry Davies was now the underwriting department manager in our New Jersey regional office. Word on the street had it that Larry was also in need of a division manager. If Bill was so determined to screw me, here was his chance to act like a man, and kiss me in the process. Sending me to New Jersey as a division manager would return me to my roots. There, I could lick my wounds and perhaps forget about his skullduggery. In closing, I told Bill that he had a week to consider his options, while I would consider filing an EEOC complaint.

Bill was no longer hemming and hawing. Although I had no intentions of filing a complaint, he could hardly afford to call my bluff. If his dastardly deed became a matter of public record, it might very well cost him dearly. The easy way out for Bill was to grant my tortured wish. He contacted me by phone while I was still out of town to advise me that Larry had requested my services.

One of the best positions you can find yourself in is working for someone whom you admire. Effective April 1, 1978, I got the chance to do just that. Despite the gloomy circumstances surrounding my move, I was heartened by the opportunity to work for an apparent superstar. And Larry didn't disappoint. We picked up where we had left off after our first encounter in Dallas, Texas.

Larry was a master at pushing me to the limit. Hard as I tried to meet his expectations, I consistently fell short of the mark. The purpose in playing this evil game with me was to teach me an important lesson. If all I could do was meet his demands without adding unique value, given my own grasp of the overarching mission, Larry would have been thoroughly unimpressed. When it finally occurred to me that doing what he wanted was the *beginning* of an assignment, I managed to earn his lukewarm approval.

Underwriting prerogatives were severely limited in New Jersey. Mandatory insurance laws required auto insurers to "take all comers" as long as prospective customers possessed a valid driver's license. Absent the ability to pick and choose business based on quality characteristics, we turned our attention toward generating proper rates, which was a never-ending battle for truth and justice.

Customers were inclined to be less than forthright about factors that influenced their premiums. Heavy losses were being incurred by auto insurers due to the excessive frequency of accidents, ambulance chasers, unscrupulous lawyers, and car thieves. Those costs were reflected in average premiums that were beginning to eat up a disproportionate share of disposable income. It was a variation of the basic themes negatively affecting health-care costs today.

In response to the rising costs of auto insurance, some hard-pressed insureds would "misrepresent" their exposure in the interest of lower premium charges. Such customers came to be known as "rate evaders," and it was my job to hunt them down. I'm not at liberty to discuss the methods used to nab these villains, because that would be the equivalent of giving away trade secrets. What I can say is that my vigilance was enough to warm the cockles of Larry's ice-cold heart.

As a way of giving me an "attaboy," Larry granted me frequent exposure to his boss, a man by the name of David B. Winn. Dave held the title of assistant regional manager, a newly created job for people being groomed to eventually become regional managers. Dave was to Larry what Larry was to me: mentor, sponsor, and friend. What we all shared in common was a career that started in underwriting, with no idea where it might lead.

I reveled in the time that I spent with Larry and Dave, but it ended much too soon. Dave moved on to become a regional manager some six months after my arrival. One month later, Larry was promoted to the position of Midwest zone underwriting manager, leaving me to feel like a motherless child. Frank Morello replaced Larry as underwriting department manager, and I would begin the process of proving myself anew.

Fortunately for me, Frank was a star in his own right, which made for an easy transition. His management style was in stark contrast to Larry's, offering me an alternate view of how to effectively approach my job. Frank was also kind enough to encourage me to keep in touch with Larry, knowing that the two of us had forged an intimate bond. From his new position in the Midwest zone, Larry was doing everything within his power to help keep me on the move.

Effective April 1, 1979, I was promoted to the position of underwriting department manager in the Indianapolis region, a proud member of the Midwest zone. It would mark the fourth time in four consecutive years that I had been relocated on April 1. It also marked my entry into middle management, where I would spend nearly fifteen years.

Mixing It Up in Middle Management

After four moves in eight and a half years, I was finally in charge of my very own department. Words can't describe how wonderful it felt to live up to Bill Gilstrap's bold prediction. It took a couple of months for the reality to sink in, and a whole lot longer to get used to the idea of living in Indianapolis. Compared to the other towns I had lived in, Indy was a bit of a burg. The single most prominent cultural event in any given year was the running of the Indy 500! But the cost of living was much to my liking, and it was a good place to raise a family.

My new boss was a regional manager by the name of C. Robert Snyder. (The C stood for Clyde, though he understandably preferred being called Bob.) Bob was a gifted businessman who had come up through the controller ranks. He knew more about making money than anyone I had ever met. In the four-plus years that I worked for Bob, he simultaneously taught me things about growing the top line, improving the bottom line, and managing expenses.

Before Bob would spend a dime's worth of time tutoring me on matters of high finance, I had to prove to him beyond the shadow of a doubt that I was more than capable of running a high-powered underwriting department.

Bob was equally demanding of every department manager. Setting high performance standards served us well, but nobody more so than Bob. By heading a region that outperformed others in the Midwest zone, he was setting himself up for *his* next promotion.

Home Office was fostering a healthy competition between regions, countrywide. At the end of each year, the four zone vice presidents were asked to select one region within their purview for recognition as "best in class." Objective measures included growth in agent head count, average premiums, gross premiums, profit margins, and loss containment. Other critical measures were employee opinion surveys and customer satisfaction.

Every department within our region was expected to toe the line. As underwriting pooh-bah, my primary focus was on programs that favorably influenced a wide variety of criteria. The first call to order was getting a good handle on the quality of new business. As with LEW for renewals, AURES was a newly created automated program that replaced the underwriters' manual review of new business applications.

AURES was the acronym for "alert underwriting risk evaluation system." A score was assigned to each piece of new business based on a combination of attendant risk factors. Scores would fall into one of three categories: high, medium, and low. The higher the score, the greater the risk. Low- and medium-score business was issued without human intervention. Only high-score applications were routinely subject to an underwriter's review.

AURES, like LEW, was held in contempt early on. Unlike LEW, there was no easy way to reconcile AURES decisions. AURES was a highly sophisticated computer program, and given the heavy volume of new business receipts, it was virtually impossible to recreate a manual review. It would take several months for me, and a math-savvy supervisor by the name of Mike Moorcroft, to decipher the essence of AURES. Once the code was broken, we could manage the quality of our new business receipts better than any other region in the country.

With new business quality under control, I could focus my attention on premium development. Average premiums were under attack due to a highly competitive auto market. The Indy region was responsible for business written in the states of Indiana and Kentucky. Unlike New Jersey, these states weren't overly regulated, nor were they burdened with the heavy losses commonly associated with densely populated urban centers.

Companies, large and small, were literally and figuratively fighting for new business. Auto insurance was turning into a commodity. The power of a company's brand now paled in comparison to the cost of its products. Under those market conditions, consumers were inclined to equate what they saw as lowest price with their idea of best value. Once that happened, more than a handful of agents, and customers alike, started to misrepresent risk characteristics to achieve the lowest possible premium, as opposed to what was fitting and proper.

The region was not inclined to tolerate such nonsense. Bob was too smart a businessman to let tainted sales devalue solid growth. (A regional manager with a sales background might have been tempted to turn a blind eye.) I was allowed to bring my New Jersey rate-evader skills to bear in the heartland of mid-America. Since Allstate was fond of using acronyms, I came up with one to introduce a new underwriting program proudly entitled LIARSS.

LIARSS, as in liars, was the hue and cry for "let's investigate all reasonably suspicious shit!" My underwriters jumped for joy at the chance to strike a mighty blow on behalf of PAR, which stood for "proper Allstate rates." The sales department took umbrage at the idea, but when Bob gave his okay, I was free to get down and dirty.

Here again, I am not at liberty to give away trade secrets. I can, however, shed a little light on how the program was managed. At the end of every month, we compiled an exhaustive list of policy numbers, representing accounts that were found to be mis-rated. In each case, we listed the amount of premium recouped, along with the agent of record. We made no attempt to lay blame on anybody. We simply let the premium adjustments do the talking.

The results were shared with Bob and the sales manager at regularly scheduled PAR meetings. At first, these meetings were long and drawn-out affairs, given the sheer volume of names on the list. After a few months, the list became smaller and smaller, as agents were getting the message that Bob was getting pissed off. Several meetings later, the problem began to resolve itself. We suspended the monthly meetings, although we continued to issue the report. It reinforced a management axiom I discovered early on; that which gets measured, gets done.

Entering my fourth year as an underwriting department manager, things were going quite well. Bob considered me a major player on his staff, and the region held the title "best in the Midwest" three consecutive years. I began looking forward to my next promotion, which would likely be as underwriting department manager in a larger and more complex region. Before that opportunity could materialize, I was confronted with a nasty situation that carried with it career-shattering consequences.

The drama unfolded against the backdrop of a Midwest zone underwriting managers' conference. These meetings were scheduled, periodically, to bring underwriting managers from around the zone together for the purpose of sharing information. The zone underwriting manager was host of the conference and responsible for setting the agenda. Larry Davies was no longer in that position, having been promoted to the Michigan region as an assistant regional manager, working for none other than the regional manager, Dave Winn. Get the picture?

Tim Brown was the current zone underwriting manager. He and I had a tenuous relationship. Jack Blackburn was the zone vice president. He was both Tim's and my boss's boss. Ted Rupley was the Home Office underwriting vice president, a two-time former regional manager, on his way to becoming a zone vice president. Jack, Ted, and Tim were the major players taking part in the conference. It was with them that I would eventually come to verbal blows.

The first three days of the conference could be described as uneventful. Nothing out of the ordinary had taken place. Most of my peers were anxious to get back home, and frankly, so was I. Getaway day was Friday, with a farewell dinner scheduled for Thursday night. Thursday afternoon was reserved for interaction with Jack, Ted, and Tim. One of the topics slated for discussion was the challenge of affirmative action. As the only person of color sitting in the room, I had a sneaky suspicion that "the shit was about to get funky."

The conversation started out innocently enough. Tim pointed out that, of the few minority department managers in the country, underwriting had two, and one was in the Midwest zone. That one would be me. It was fine for us to be proud of that distinction, but there was a long way to go before achieving the appropriate mix of minority and women department managers. The biggest challenge facing us as leaders was the limited number of qualified candidates presently in the pipeline.

As managers, we needed to do a better job of identifying and grooming minorities and women with middle- and upper-management potential. That sounded more than reasonable to me. What didn't sound reasonable was the stuff that followed. Tim observed that, as he traveled around the regions within the zone, he hadn't met more than one or two minority or female supervisors who seemed qualified to move beyond their current positions.

As a matter of fact, in talking with his fellow zone-underwriting managers, all three of whom were white males, they came to the conclusion that there was a shortage of affirmative-action talent throughout the entire country. I found such claims hard to believe. With Jack in the room, and the session being interactive, I asked him what he was doing from his seat of great power to promote affirmative action.

Seven Midwest zone regional managers reported directly to him, as well as seven zone department managers. Surely, he was in a position to force the issue, assuming he truly believed in the cause. Jack told the group that he didn't have the power to look into a man's soul to determine if he embraced affirmative action as a corporate strategy. All he could do was encourage his people to "do the right thing," like he was doing in this meeting. As I listened to Jack speak, I was stunned by the dim-witted nature of his response.

Not to be out-dumbed, Ted decided to open his mouth. He shared with the group a story about a recent encounter of his with managers from around the country who were participating in a management workshop called "Colleagues in Action." These managers were from different departments and regions, including zone and Home Office personnel. They represented the most diverse cross-section of lower-management talent in the company.

One of the group exercises they participated in was breaking out into smaller groups based on gender and race. They ended up in groups of four: males and females, black and white. Each group was then sent to a separate room where the members were asked to list on a flip chart values that were important to them in their lives, both at home and at work. After completing the assignment, the groups were reunited in one room and asked to reveal their list of values.

Ted said that he was fascinated by the results. According to him, the value systems of white males, white females, and *even black females*, were almost identical. They believed in a higher being or authority; they believed in working hard; they believed in raising their children; they believed in playing by the rules. Ted went on to say, "The only thing black males cared about was being cool, dressing cool, and driving big cars." He actually said this out loud!

Needless to say, all eyes were on me, but I chose to play invisible. I thought it best to bite my tongue and swallow a river of blood before opening my mouth and letting it flow. But Tim Brown was not about to let me off that easy. Everyone in the room sensed that I was seething. Tim observed, on behalf of the group, that it was odd, if not disturbing, to see me sit in silence. Surely, as a member of the "protected class," I had something to add to this conversation.

My instincts told me that Tim was setting me up. He knew from past experience that I was opinionated, usually more than willing to express a provocative point of view. But in this case, I ran the risk of insulting "the ruling class," which might result in a death sentence of sorts. Before I could think through it all, their bullshit got the best of me. That's when I took a deep breath, said a silent prayer, and proceeded to damn the torpedoes.

For the next twenty minutes, I engaged in a verbal assault of my own, starting with a rejoinder to Tim's allegations. His assertion that upwardly mobile affirmative-action candidates were in short supply failed to address the specific skills sets that minorities and women lacked. Were we hiring folks not smart enough, tall enough, skinny enough, or what? Without the benefit of knowing what he considered deficient in the hiring practices of affirmative-action candidates, how on earth could he expect us to stop shooting ourselves in the foot? Or maybe he thought we were hiring minorities and women who weren't sufficiently "white male" enough!

Tim was left to solve this riddle while I turned my attention to Jack. I suggested that peering into the soul of mankind had nothing to do with his ability to support affirmative action. All he had to do was hold his staff accountable for getting results in affirmative action, as he did with any other corporate mandate. If one of his regional managers failed to grow the business, he could replace that person with someone who would. If one of his managers failed to promote affirmative action, he could replace that person with someone who would. Accepting failure should not be an option. I told Jack he needed to check his own soul for affirmative action to flourish.

The last person left for me to redress was Ted, and I would take great pleasure in doing so. Ted's offhanded comments were easily the most egregious and came as no particular surprise. He had a well-earned reputation for being an arrogant son of a bitch, and we had crossed swords once before. Given the tone and tenor of what I had said thus far, there was very little left for me to lose.

I told Ted that I initially found his "Colleagues" anecdote offensive. It put me in mind of racial epithets, along the lines of calling black men lazy and shiftless. Then it occurred to me that Ted *had me in mind* when he was being so recklessly cavalier. Regardless of Ted's motives, or lack thereof, taking his comments personally was clearly the right thing to do. Ted's only crime was failing to see "the forest for the trees," if not missing the point altogether.

Of everyone seated within the sound of Ted's voice, I alone stood guilty as charged of "being cool, dressing cool, and driving a big car." Ted should have been thankful for that. Had I not been cool as he deigned to engage in stereotyped drivel, I would have straightened my silk tie (with the matching pocket square), stood up from my chair, spit in his face, left the building, gotten into my Cadillac Coupe De Ville, and driven my black ass back to Indy.

None of those supposed black male predilections negatively affected my ability to do the job. My underwriting results were consistently better than any of my peers, which had something to do with the Indy region being "best in the Midwest," year after year after year. I told Ted that what should "fascinate" him was meeting with people, minorities and women included, who were helping the company prosper. Then check for value systems that *they* shared in common. And when he was finished doing that, he should follow up with Tim to see how he was doing with the assignment I had given him.

What you just read was the sanitized version of my profanity-laced diatribe. This meeting sent shock waves throughout the entire Allstate complex in less than twenty-four hours. Before I could get back to the office on Monday morning to tell my boss what had happened, Jack had already reached him by phone and given him an earful. That's the only thing that really bothered me, reflecting poorly on Bob.

I gave Bob a full account of what had transpired, in all its gory detail. To his everlasting credit, Bob told me not to sweat it. But he did acknowledge that damage had been done, and for that, I would be put in "the penalty box." My career was in need of rehabilitation. Bob promised to do whatever he could to help me make amends. By the same token, I wanted Bob to know that if I ever found myself in a similar situation again, I would probably react the same way.

For me, it was a simple matter of speaking truth to power when the stakes were too high to do otherwise. Granted, it was wrong for me to do so in anger. It would be wrong for you as well. But I'm a firm believer in being painfully honest with people, including the boss, when the situation warrants it. You should handle these conversations with tact and diplomacy. The timing of these conversations should also be taken into account. Finally, you should never speak truth to power for the sheer pleasure of suggesting that "the emperor has no clothes."

I would begin the process of rehabilitation by extending olive braches and offering mea culpas. I called Jack and apologized for causing a scene. He graciously accepted my apology. I called Tim and offered to set up an affirmative-action workshop in the Midwest zone. He graciously declined my offer. Before I could make amends with Ted, rumors had it that he had been asked to "take a hike" on the grounds of being an asshole. What got me back in good graces as much as anything else was continuing to do an outstanding job. And my good friend and colleague, Larry Davies, would extend a helping hand yet again.

As of early 1983, Larry was regional manager in Michigan, replacing Dave Winn, who had since moved on to become president of our Canadian company. Effective August 1, 1983, I was promoted to the Michigan region and became Larry's underwriting manager. A lot had changed since he and I had worked together in New Jersey. I was getting divorced, thanks in part to the onset of careerism. I was more focused on being a boss than a husband. My wife was more focused on being a mother than a wife. In the end, the two of us got what we wanted. It broke my heart that our daughter had to pay a certain price.

As a single head of household, I was totally free to work hard and play harder. Larry and I continued to forge a bond the likes of which continued to build my corporate muscle. Michigan was a region with lots of problems. We were hemorrhaging red ink, annually, to the tune of losses in excess of twenty million dollars. Most of our losses were related to maintaining a large book of business in the city of Detroit. The auto book of business was the biggest drain on assets, but the homeowner's book wasn't much better.

The root cause of our problems had to do with urban decay. Industry was fleeing to the surrounding suburban bands of Detroit, taking with it jobs, revenues, and hope. As soon as the city's infrastructure started to crumble, insurance regulators imposed civic-minded authority to keep insurance companies from abandoning the city. Premium increases were effectively held in check and severe restraints were placed on sound underwriting practices, making it virtually impossible for a company like Allstate, which was the biggest provider of insurance in the city, to do anything but "lose their shirts, and parts of their hips."

We were barely able to keep our fiscal head above water. Senior management in Home Office was rumored to be drawing up plans to withdraw our license from the state, thereby cutting our losses and shutting down operations. At the same time, insurance department officials were drawing up plans of their own to block our exit strategy. Things were a mess, but as long as I had Larry in the trenches with me, I looked forward to each day on the job.

A year or so after grinding it out in Michigan, Larry was promoted to our Canadian operation; you guessed it, replacing Dave Winn as president. Larry was replaced by someone completely unknown to me, a gentleman by the name of Ed Young. This would be only the second time that Ed worked in a region. Most of his career had been spent working in Home Office. Ed was a member of FCAS, a fellow of the casualty actuarial society.

I didn't have a clue as to what that said about Ed. In very short order, I came to the realization that he was one of the smartest people on planet Earth. I mourned the loss of Larry to Canada. But in terms of what Ed brought to the table, it was, "*Au revoir*, Larry, don't let the door...!"

I'm teasing when I say that about Larry. Were it not for him, Ed and I would have never met. Larry had my back, in good times and bad, throughout my lower- and middle-management career. Ed would take his place as my rock of Gibraltar during my upper-management career. (Larry and I are still thick as thieves, along with our Allstate brides here in sunny south Florida. We will remain so for the rest of our lives.) Dave Winn would also be there for me, but I'm getting ahead of myself.

Ed was taking the helm of a sinking ship, as far as I could tell, yet he seemed glad to be aboard. In very short order, it became quite apparent that he was more than up to the task. Ed set sail for safe harbor, steering the ship with a slow and steady hand. Under his brilliant leadership, the region reversed its losing trend and managed to generate an annual profit of twenty-three million dollars in less than two short years.

Several key factors made for Ed's success, not the least of which was his gargantuan brain and intellectual firepower. Ed was what you might call an insurance savant. His actuarial training enabled him to plumb the depths of

Michigan's onerous insurance code. P.A.145, as the code was known, left very little wiggle room for insurance companies to price and underwrite their products. The code was intended to make insurance affordable after making it mandatory. This was a noble gesture on the part of insurance regulators, but it thoroughly confused traditional rate-making logic, while putting the kibosh on reliable underwriting practices.

A man by the name of Richard J. Haayen was chairman of Allstate at the time. Dick came up through the underwriting ranks, so he was keenly aware of what we were up against. He also knew about Ed's unique talent, which was why he had hand-picked Ed for the job. Ed was effectively reporting directly to Dick, and therefore had access to unlimited resources. He was put on a short leash to either fix the problems or recommend pulling the plug.

Ed didn't need much time or help solving our pricing dilemma. He designed a pricing strategy that revolutionized our way of setting rates in Michigan, the core of which is still in use today. He did, however, need a considerable amount of help in redressing our underwriting issues. That's where I came in. Inspired by Ed's novel approach to pricing, I sought to make radical changes to underwriting policies and procedures. Some of these changes were extreme to the point of making Ed uncomfortable.

The first change I lobbied for was to require our agents to submit color photos, front and back, of homes they were seeking to insure. This would significantly reduce our exposure to properties that lacked pride of ownership or proper maintenance. It would also reduce our exposure to fraud. We typically paid inspection companies to perform this task, but by getting our agents involved before closing the deal, we cut our expenses and avoided potential losses.

The most sweeping change I lobbied for was to re-structure our homeowner contracts. Replacement-cost policies were the industry standard, but market conditions were forcing me to rethink our position. We had quite a few homes on the books for which replacement costs, in the event of a substantial or total loss, were significantly higher than their market value. The problem with this phenomenon was easy to understand but devilishly hard to fix.

Under normal market conditions, the market value of a home is consistent with the cost to replace it. Replacement-cost policies are, therefore, priced to contemplate expected losses in line with market values. Where you run into problems is when replacement costs associated with claims are consistently higher than market values. That was the root cause of our problems in Detroit. The market value of homes was under considerable downward pressure. Making matters worse was the scarcity of building materials that were commonly used in Detroit's housing stock at the turn of the twentieth century.

Replacement-cost policies were no longer a proper fit for many of our homeowner customers living in Detroit. We had to identify homes that were best served by a market value policy, and make the switch without causing undue concern. Given the political realities, insurance regulators would have to approve our bold action, and were understandably reluctant to do so. Oddly enough, no one else would be more concerned with my recommendation than I.

Detroit's population was predominantly black. There was a very good chance that community leaders would look at Allstate's business decision as being racially motivated. If they didn't, the local media surely would. Once it got wind of what we were thinking, local TV news coverage made it the lead story: *Allstate gearing up to redline!*

Who will save the city? Roving reporters were dispatched to the regional office demanding on-camera interviews with company officials. Since it was my idea as the underwriting manager, I was chosen to "fade the heat."

It didn't hurt that the company front man turned out to be a black guy. Nor did it hurt that I took full ownership for the company's plan and could explain it in compassionate terms. In less than a week, I did three on-camera interviews with each of the local affiliates for ABC, NBC, and CBS news. I also appeared on a *Good Morning Detroit*-style local TV program to discuss the business case and anticipated customer benefits. In spite of our robust public relations campaign, regulators remained unconvinced.

Intense negotiations began between Home Office, the region, Governor James Blanchard, and the insurance commissioner's office. Dick Haayen had our general counsel, Bob Pike, get involved along with a coterie of attorneys. There I was, smack-dab in the middle of it all, making the case that this was a fair and equitable solution to an undeniably bad situation. Allstate prevailed because it had the law on its side. Ed pinned the credit largely on me.

This was the most exhilarating experience of my life, next to the birth of my child and that first date with an old flame named Peggy. Shortly after Ed arrived on the scene, there was no such thing as "business as usual." Ed didn't report to the Midwest zone vice president; he reported to the chairman's office. Our Monday morning staff meetings often took place out of town at corporate headquarters in Northbrook, Illinois.

Normally, we flew commercial. The flight between Detroit and Chicago's O'Hare was less than thirty minutes. A seven a.m. departure time usually landed us in Dick's boardroom no later than nine a.m. When Dick was pressed for time, he sent the corporate jet to deliver us at his convenience. A chartered helicopter picked us up from a private hangar at Midway airport and dropped us off on the landing pad in front of Home Office. Talk about arriving in style!

We met with Dick and key members of his staff, who were interested in what we called a "status report." The status report was a detailed outline of each auto and homeowner problem we faced, and every initiative we were pursuing to fix them. Dick wanted to know whether we had good reason to believe that we could ever turn a profit in Michigan. We told him we thought so, and we did.

I was awestruck by Ed's stewardship over the course of our excellent adventure. He gave every indication that he was, likewise, enamored of me. What I would lobby for next was a promotion to Home Office as an underwriting director. Ed intimated that he saw the logic, but he cautioned me to cool my jets. Dave Winn, who was now Midwest zone vice president, saw my immediate future differently. According to Ed, Dave wanted me to serve another stint as an underwriting department manager.

This came as a huge disappointment. After everything I had done to put the state of Michigan back on the map, how could they do this to me? Ed tried to console me by saying Dave thought the world of me, dating back to our days in New Jersey. Now Dave was faced with major underwriting challenges in the state of Illinois. Given what I had accomplished in Michigan, Dave thought I was "the only man for the job." Uh-oh!

Effective February 1, 1986, I was "promoted" to the Illinois region as underwriting manager. George Bender was the regional manager, which made him my new boss. Like so many of his brethren, George had made his mark in the sales department during a period of unbridled growth. But, just as my former boss George Cobb had predicted, the pendulum was swinging back. Bottom-line results were now the rage, and apparently George Bender didn't get the memo. Dave wanted me to infiltrate the region and literally keep an eye on George. Yikes!

This sounded like an affront to everything I believed in, from Jesus Christ to the Holy Ghost. What manner of unholy alliance was Dave putting forth? It sounded like a setup to me, wherein I ran the risk of being snared, *by George!* Dave tried to assure me that his proposal was on the up and up. Rather than being some grand conspiracy, Dave was simply asking me to help George see the light with respect to improving the region's bottom-line results. He also advised me that George, himself, would probably be on the move—and soon.

Dave was pulling all the strings—mine, Ed's, George's, and the region's. I had to accept his shadowy terms, though I did so with great reservation. This was hardly what I would call a plum assignment, but there comes a time when a good corporate soldier is asked to take a bullet for the team. This was one of those times. Dave sent me packing into the breach with a solemn promise that my sacrifice would not go unrewarded. I told Dave I would follow him to the gates of hell if he failed to keep his promise, another case of speaking truth to power.

Working for George wasn't nearly as bad as I had imagined. He was a warm, outgoing man with a pleasant disposition who treated his staff quite well. But George was a salesman, through and through, who chose to ignore the realities of his marketplace and the company's new direction. George was trapped in the "old school." He thought we could sell our way out of any problem. That's the belief that had been drilled into him for more than thirty years. To a large extent, I felt sorry for George. His only crime was sticking to his guns.

George may have been old school, but he was certainly nobody's fool. He knew that Dave was leery of him, and that he should be leery of me. Two months after I settled into the job, George summoned me to his office and asked me to close the door. He also told his secretary that we were not to be disturbed. I braced myself for an onslaught that never materialized. George would resort to killing me softly instead, by informing me that he was aware of my little secret.

George accused me of being Dave's informant, or worse still, a Home Office plant. George said that, in either case, he didn't trust me. Neither did his sales managers. Unless I wanted to get fired on the spot, I had best keep in mind that I worked for him and him alone. Without so much as even furrowing his brow, George slowly rose from behind his desk, opened the door, and told me to have a good day.

It was all I could do to keep from shitting a brick. The only thing stopping me was George's big foot up my ass. I had gone from conquering hero in Michigan to arch villain in Illinois. My next inclination was to seek and hide behind Dave, but that would have been a cowardly act. The only thing left for me to do was face the music like a man. I went about doing my job to the best of my ability without deference to Dave or George. If that wasn't good enough to satisfy both, I would happily die with my boots on.

Not one to hold a grudge, George slowly but surely embraced my underwriting philosophy. Before we had a chance to become bosom buddies, George was shipped off to Home Office, just like Dave had predicted. What Dave didn't predict was that George would be replaced by someone I took to be a preternatural force of sinister evil that went by the name of Bob Gary. As far as I could tell at the time, Bob sprang from the loins of Satan.

Allstate's senior management had a totally different view of Bob, and to be perfectly honest, I could see why. He was a ruggedly handsome man, with an athletic build and dark complexion that looked good in a business suit. In addition to that, Bob was a damn good businessman. He started his career in the sales department and moved through various sales management positions before taking on the role of regional manager in the Denver and Florida regions. Whatever Bob touched turned to gold, as far as sales results were concerned.

Bob had no interest in being a three-time regional manager, much like I had no interest in being a three-time underwriting manager. But just like me, Bob was being asked to take a bullet for the team by his sponsor, a gentleman by the name of Jerry Choate. Jerry was an executive vice president at the time and would later become chairman of the board. Bob would follow Jerry's order and later become president of our personal lines company.

Bob made no attempt to hide his displeasure with being assigned to the Illinois region. When I extended my hand to welcome him, he avoided contact, as if I had the plague. When I tried to introduce him to members of the underwriting department, he refused to make a sound. After laboring through three one-way conversations, I decided to dispense with the pleasantries and ushered Bob back to his office. Not before or since have I ever met anyone so hell-bent on being mean and nasty.

As far as working for Bob was concerned, I had no immediate complaints. He and I were on the exact same page in terms of restoring the balance between growth and profit. Bob gave me freedom to strengthen underwriting practices while he restored law and order in the sales department. Bob's reign of terror lasted only six months. He was promptly promoted to the position of territorial vice president, which was what we used to call zone vice presidents. Given the effects of a corporate reorganization, the four zones were replaced by three territories, and Bob would be in charge of one.

Replacing Bob as Illinois regional manager was a drop-dead gorgeous, minority female by the name of Rita Wilson. Rita, like Bob, was being sponsored by Jerry Choate. When I wasn't under the spell of Rita's beauty, I was listening to her tell long-winded stories about how Jerry hung the moon. She was easily one of his biggest fans, and he was no less smitten with her. Rita picked up from where Bob left off, while I continued handling my underwriting affairs. Six months later, Rita was replaced by someone named Ed Dixon, whom I remembered fondly from my days in the Indy region.

Ed served a brief stint as regional sales manager during my extended stay. He left there to become regional sales manager in the Kansas City region before being assigned to Illinois as regional manager. This sort of extraordinary fast-tracking was compliments of Jerry Choate. In less than eighteen months, I had worked for three different regional managers, all of whom were sponsored by Jerry. (If life were fair, I'd have rightfully been one of "Jerry's kids," as well!)

Two months after Ed arrived, I finally got promoted to the position of director in Home Office underwriting, working for Larry Davies, who by now was the underwriting vice president. Dave Winn was also working in Home Office, as what, I don't recall. What I do know is that he, Jerry, and several others were in a death match for the ultimate prize of being named president of Allstate. This brings me to perhaps the most valuable lesson I can leave you with: when the elephants dance, watch your toes.

The elephant dance has several different meanings. The one I refer to deals with infighting, which commonly takes place in the upper echelons of Corporate America. When I got to Home Office as underwriting director, such a dance was taking place between several people with whom I had a distant relationship. Wayne Heiden was the chairman, and Ray Keifer was president. Jerry Choate was in charge of Home Office external affairs, and Jack Callahan was in charge of internals.

I never had close contact with any of these executives but was associated with people who did. Dave Winn and Larry Davies reported to Ray Keifer, and Ed Young reported to Jack Callahan. Bob Gary, Rita Wilson, and Ed Dixon reported to Jerry Choate. This was the assembled cast of characters who would influence the remainder of my career.

How I chose to interact with these folk ultimately sealed my fate. Had I chosen to do things differently, there's no doubt in my mind that this story of mine might have a different ending. Whether it would have been happier is something I'll never know. That notwithstanding, what's important for you to appreciate is the ramifications that flow from *your* interactions. Should you be lucky enough to work with elephants, pay strict attention to the rest of my story.

A lot had changed in the twelve years that had passed since my first tour of duty in Home Office. Bill Morris was gone; I occupied his old position and worked for someone I trusted implicitly. The only thing better than going to work in the morning was coming home to my lady at night. When we first met, her last name was Bliss, which suited her to a T, as in Thomas. She was the sales manager's secretary when I arrived in Michigan. After moving to the Illinois region, she showed up on my doorstep one year later, and we've been together ever since.

No longer was I running around the country, from region to region, as a part of underwriting reviews. Now my days were spent helping design underwriting programs for implementation, countrywide. These programs were born out of a collaborative effort between many different functions. Sales was always part of the mix, along with pricing, legal, and systems. My life revolved around scheduling and attending meetings that were meant to build consensus.

Trying to build consensus among disparate groups with conflicting interests proved to be both time-consuming and mentally exhausting. When and if consensus was finally reached, it was normally over the objections of more than one person. Technical expertise would often play second fiddle to political maneuvering. And heaven forbid aligning yourself with a cause that placed a burden on sales. You did so at the risk of becoming *persona non grata*.

The nature of my job put me in this awkward position on a regular basis, but I gladly accepted the challenge. Every sponsor who played a major role in my development was doing the same. If they could do it, I could do it and stand by their side. Ed Young was first to have me join him on the firing line. He was taking aim at an auto initiative that sales would find problematic. The bone of contention was whether to include credit reports as a part of our underwriting review. Sales saw it as an impediment to growth. We saw it as adding value to risk selection.

The ebb and flow of constant debate was our steady diet in Home Office. Jerry and his troops were determined to grow at a steady pace, while Dave and his troops insisted on solid profits. In the interest of self-preservation, I needed to develop a communications style that could effectively serve both camps. What I decided to do was frame our debates while taking advantage of technology. It allowed me to create colorful presentations that put the pros and cons of everyone's ideas in the most favorable light.

Today's technology makes that idea seem passé. In the mid to late '80s, it was anything but. People were so taken by my carefully crafted 35-mm slide presentations that they were willing to put aside their preconceived notions and start thinking outside the box. Not every debate was settled on this score, but at least our discussions were considerably less hostile, and therefore more productive.

Over the course of several months, I had established myself as the go-to guy for people in my department who needed to make a presentation. Larry was so impressed with my particular skills that he asked me to put together his presentations for use in meetings where I wasn't invited! I was more than happy to oblige. Not nearly as happy as when Dave Winn suddenly offered me the job of assistant vice president. Less than a year after returning to Home Office, I had reached the highest level of middle management.

Dave's job offer came on the heels of the company's latest and greatest reorganization. Personal lines were being split between two distinctive groups. One group would handle auto lines of insurance. The other group would concentrate on property lines. Dave Winn was named president of the property group, and he chose me to be his underwriting vice president. I was now an appointed officer of Allstate Insurance who, by virtue of this title, got a luxury company car, an oversized office, and hefty stock-option grants in excess of my annual salary. I also got access to the corporate jet, the officers' dining room, and luxury condos located in New York City, Washington, DC, and London, England.

Not one to rest on my laurels, I was anxious to show Dave that he had made a wise choice. I would take full advantage of my presentation skills to introduce his new organization, countrywide. We published the equivalent of a *Look Magazine* exposé, which featured pictures and quotes from key members of Dave's new leadership group. Dave led off with a mission statement on behalf of the group, followed by mini mission statements from his assistant vice presidents. Copies of the glossy publication were sent in abundant supply to management personnel throughout the regions and Home Office.

No one was more impressed than Ray Keifer. He ordered Rex Davis, Dave's auto counterpart, to do the same on behalf of his organization. Theirs was a mirror image of our publication, with the exception of the photos and mission statements. A month had passed before their news was fit to print and ready for distribution. By the time it arrived, people took it for what it was worth, the copy of a good idea. Since imitation is the highest form of flattery, Dave knew enough to be proud as a peacock, which simultaneously feathered my nest.

There was very little time to bask in our glory before getting down to more serious business. Homeowner average premiums were once again under pressure, due to heavy competition. Policies were being issued for slightly less than their full replacement cost in order to reduce premium charges. A replacement cost "guaranty" built into all replacement-cost contracts had the effect of protecting the customers' interest at the expense of proper Allstate rates. Remember PAR?

In the interest of preserving rate integrity, I lobbied on behalf of instituting a countrywide program known as ITV, an acronym for "insurance to value." The mechanics of the program placed a heavy burden on agents throughout the country. Instead of binding coverage over the phone, sight unseen, agents would now be required to personally inspect properties, take photos, and measure square footage.

Photos and measurements would then be submitted to underwriting departments to confirm replacement costs.

Bob Gary was none too happy with my proposal, but Jerry Choate would have the final say. We were successful in getting Jerry to endorse the idea, and he ordered his territorial vice presidents to implement ITV. Two out of three territorial vice presidents took ownership for ITV and communicated with their regional vice presidents, formerly called regional managers. Bob Gary did no such thing. He had me introduce the program to his regional vice presidents. By putting me out front, Bob's regional vice presidents knew that ITV was being implemented over his dead body.

A come to Jesus meeting was scheduled to take place in a conference room at the LAX Hilton in Los Angeles, California. Bob knew better than anyone that the meeting held potential to be spirited. He assured me that he would back my play in the face of violent objections. Since Jerry had placed his imprimatur on the program, I had reason to believe that I could trust Bob to keep his word. But when the bullets started flying, as we both knew they would, Bob was conspicuously missing in action.

Rather than cover me and rein in his troops, Bob was content to let me twist in the wind. Were it not for the fact that I believed in my cause, I would have told them all to kiss my ass. Discretion, arguably, being the better part of valor was why I suffered their slings and arrows, including some that were hurled by Bob. Six hours later, the dust was finally starting to settle. Before I could bring the meeting to a close, an earthquake shook the rafters. Because it measured less than five on the Richter scale, I suggested to my audience that this was God's way of saying, "ITV is a small force of nature."

As we winged our way back home on the corporate jet, Bob acknowledged that he had gone MIA. Consistent with my diagnosis of his bipolarity, the comment was at once satisfying and disconcerting. Bob had known full well that he would go AWOL, which was probably part of his evil plan from the get-go. What he failed to realize was that I didn't want or need him in my foxhole. As long as Jerry was calling the shots, there was nothing Bob or his regional vice presidents could do to keep from installing ITV.

Whether it was lobbying on behalf of the use of credit reports or implementing ITV, I got the distinct feeling I was getting under Bob's skin. Maybe it had more to do with me, personally, than it did my business pursuits. In any case, I could tell I wasn't one of Bob's favorite people, and he surely wasn't one of mine. As long as I was in the good graces of Dave, Larry, and Ed, I was okay with our mutual contempt.

I continued plugging along for a couple of years when Rita Wilson, who was a territorial vice president at the time, approached me. She offered me a job as regional vice president, which under normal circumstances would have been the next logical step in my progression. Unfortunately, the circumstances were far from normal, making for a hitch in our get along.

The region in question was an operations center, which was a hybrid form of regional office. There were no traditional departments in regional operations centers, or ROCs, as they were called, like sales, underwriting, claims, etc. The company was pioneering a new approach to processing applications outside the realm of these endeavors. The primary functions contained in ROCs were mail processing, billing, and customer service, things in which I had no interest, let alone expertise.

Making matters worse was Rita's estimation that the ROC she would have me lead probably needed to be closed. The only thing more dismal than its processing was said to be employee morale. What Rita envisioned was me taking over and, in less than a year, pronouncing the ROC "DOA." But the fatal flaw in Rita's plan was the prospect of me working with my fiancée who, at the time, was the incumbent regional vice president's secretary!

Carried to its furthest logical conclusion, Rita's proposal ended with me working myself out of a job, not before firing my significant other. I told Rita I had no interest in this sort of promotional opportunity, and she appreciated my consternation. To assuage my concerns, she assured me that by accepting her offer, my future would be secure, assuming I successfully completed the mission. Furthermore, she would find a comparable job elsewhere for my fiancée, Connie, before having me make the move.

All things considered, I still wasn't thrilled with her proposal. I thought I could serve the company best by carrying on in my current assignment. To my way of thinking, it clearly involved more high-minded matters than shutting down a failed operation. Surely, Rita could find someone else who would see the ROC job as a fulfilling, if not rewarding, opportunity. Rita countered by asking me to take the job as a favor to her, which changed the dynamics completely.

The decision I faced at this point was a lot more personal. For reasons not totally clear to me, Rita considered me the best man for the job. This was somewhat different than calling me the only man for the job, which I told you once before is cock and bull. If I had it to do over again, I would have accepted Rita's terms. After all, it was a promotion, albeit one of a jaded nature. More importantly, Rita was not only offering me a job, she was offering herself up as a sponsor. The best "do as I say, not as I do" advice I can give you is as follows: never deny an elephant's request to sponsor you; it's the equivalent of stepping on its toes.

After several weeks of negotiating with Dave, Rita, and Rita's boss, I managed to turn down Rita's offer without doing irreparable damage. I say this because little more than a year later Rita approached me with another proposition, intended to broaden my horizons. There are a few other matters which need to be discussed before getting to that proposition.

The landscape was beginning to change, ever so slightly, within the ranks of senior management. The elephant dance had people moving to and fro, with Dave Winn caught in the mix. He was being replaced by someone named Ray Tibbitts, or "three T's, two B's, two I's, and an S," as we joked behind his back. (It was a dyslexic way of spelling his last name.) Ray had an underwriting background that gave me something to work with in terms of accepting him as my new lord and master. And it didn't hurt, either, when Dave told Ray that I would prove to be one of his most valuable assets. It took awhile for the two of us to click, but when we did, I was good to go.

As we approached the property group's third anniversary in the spring of '91, some cause for alarm came to our attention, which required Ray Keifer's consideration. Through the use of sophisticated modeling techniques, our research center located in Menlo Park, California, advised us that we were overexposed in Florida and California. "Too much of a good thing" was another way to look at our sad situation. With the amount of homeowner business we had on the books in those two states, a category four hurricane here, or a Richter scale seven earthquake there, would leave us in dire straits.

"There's a turd in the punch bowl!" was not the sort of message we were anxious to deliver. Still, someone needed to do the dirty deed, and I quickly volunteered to be the messenger. Odds were in favor of the messenger getting killed, but the daunting task of speaking truth to power was getting to be a habit with me. I put forth a down and dirty presentation that colorfully portrayed the calamitous financial impacts of a "one in a hundred years" natural disaster.

To underscore how volatile senior managements' blowback might be, Ray Tibbitts scheduled the meeting to take place on a day he also had set aside to undergo minor surgery. John Drennan was the resident expert within the property group, who, as vice president of pricing and a full fellow actuary, was qualified to address any technical questions surrounding the use of models. As assistant vice president of property underwriting, I would handle any other flak.

Ray Keifer was joined by Jerry Choate, Bob Gary, Ed Young, and several others. After our guests were comfortably seated, we dimmed the lights, turned on the projector, and launched into our tale of woe. From my vantage point in the darkened room, it was hard to see people's faces. I did however hear, over the sound of my voice, the weeping and gnashing of teeth. There was no way to tell who was doing what, but I could feel the heat of Bob Gary's glare on the back of my neck and shoulders.

I had to be careful not to pass judgment on us being caught with our pants down. There were people in the room who were partially responsible, and I was loath to point an accusing finger. Jerry had set records in California as an agent and sales manager. Bob had set sales records in

Florida when he was regional manager. The most we could do was lay objective facts on the table and let Ray Keifer and his staff take them under advisement.

The only thing of consequence to happen shortly after the meeting was another corporate reorganization, which resulted in the property group's disbandment. I'm not suggesting a connection between the two. I'll let you draw your own conclusions. The auto and property functions were reunited. My dear friend Larry Davies could no longer serve as underwriting vice president due to his failing health. He was forced into early retirement and eventually replaced by Frank Morello.

History was now repeating itself. Once again, Frank took Larry's place; and once again, the transition was silky smooth. But other management changes associated with the reorganization were the source of some concern. Jerry Choate put Bob Gary in charge of external affairs (growth) and Ed Young in charge of internal affairs (profit). Much to my professional and personal dismay, Dave Winn was put out to pasture.

In one fell swoop, my two staunchest supporters, Larry and Dave, were nowhere to be found. In taking their leave, they also took with them a large measure of my job security. I still had Frank, who reported to Ed, and for their sake as well as my own, I would keep on keeping on. With my head kept down, and nose to the grindstone, I steered clear of Bob Gary, and prayed no harm would come to me. My prayers were answered in six short months, when Ed Young offered me the position of vice president of Product Administration, effective October 1, 1993.

Down and Out in Upper Management

At long last, I was master of my own domain and feeling pretty good about myself. Out of forty thousand-plus employees countrywide, only fifty at a time could be elected officers as designated by an outside board of directors. Their entry-level position was vice president, and they were respectfully referred to as the "Nifty Fifty." What marked the occasion as especially sweet was being the very first minority male ever to join the ranks of elected officers. The icing on the cake was finally gaining access to a hallowed corner office.

My first corner office was a luxurious home away from home, even more spacious than my one-bedroom apartment in the heart of downtown Chicago. Furnishings included a tasteful assortment of couches, chairs, cabinets, end tables, cocktail tables, an armoire, and plants. My desk was large enough to seat three people, but only accommodated one high-backed chair. The wall-to-wall carpeting, bay windows, and artwork provided the finishing touches.

To be honest, I would have settled for the executive secretary's office, which was attached to mine by a common wall. It was one-third the size but no less richly appointed, and served as cozy buffer between me and the outside world. In order to get to me, you had to get past my secretary, whose primary job was to protect the king at all costs. No matter how bad things got at home or at work, if I could just get to my corner office, all was right with the world.

The job itself was very much to my liking. As vice president of Product Administration, I was responsible for the oversight and maintenance of all policies sold within the personal lines company. Any contract changes required by state law or regulation came through our shop, as well as requests by the field to modify policies due to competitive pressures or market conditions.

Forever intrigued by the notion of changing the world or reinventing the wheel, I could barely contain myself. There was any number of game-changing ideas which I encouraged the enterprise to consider. "I'd like (X amount) of dollars' worth of insurance, please!" struck me as best of them all. As opposed to forcing our customers to buy multiple lines of insurance (auto, home, life) at prices we set, why not let them set the price according to their budget needs? Then we, as the insurance experts, could design a single master policy based on their household exposure.

Nearly all of my bright ideas were overwhelmed by senior management's lack of interest. The general impression I got from them was "if it ain't broke, don't fix it." But that didn't dissuade me from tilting at windmills. I believed in what I was doing, and I was having too much fun. Ed Young had provided me with this opportunity of a lifetime and I would forever be indebted to him. And it's that neverending devotion to Ed that brings me back to Rita.

When I last spoke of Rita, she was on the verge of making me another offer. Surely, I wouldn't be so cataclysmically stupid as to spurn her a second time around. Or would I?

Instead of offering me a job in her role as sponsor, Rita was now playing the role of mentor. And what she had to offer was advice, the kind that made me sick to my stomach. As a charter member of Jerry Choate's inner circle, Rita had access to privileged information. According to her, major organizational changes were about to unfold, which she knew would have a bearing on my future prospects. While keeping Jerry's trust, Rita went on to tell me in so many words that I needed to start kissing Bob Gary's ass.

Before I could tell her that she had lost her beautiful mind, Rita hit me with two more deathblows. She implied that my longtime sponsor and friend, Dave Winn, was about to be taken from the pasture and "put down." She further implied that my beloved Ed Young would take Dave's place in the pasture. Just as I was about to lose consciousness, Rita took my hand, squeezed it ever so softly, and assured me that everything was going to be alright.

If everything was going to be alright, Rita had to be all wrong. Rather than insult her intelligence, I asked Rita if I could question her assumptions. She obliged. I was willing to concede the fact that Jerry Choate would one day replace Ray Keifer as president of Allstate. Everyone in senior management agreed that Jerry was the best man for the job. But as for who would replace Jerry as president of personal lines, that, I argued, was open for debate.

I agreed that the two likely candidates were indeed Bob Gary and Ed Young. But from my selfish point of view, the obvious choice was Ed. Ed had forgotten more about insurance than what Jerry and Bob would ever know, combined. Throughout his career in upper management, Ed had been saddled with the toughest assignments, which he invariably handled with great aplomb. If the job was considered "mission impossible," Ed Young was the go-to guy.

Bob Gary, on the other hand, got things done through fear tactics and intimidation. Throughout his career in upper management, Bob became known as the prince of darkness, while people on his staff came to be known as children of the damned. I found it hard if not impossible to believe that Jerry would entrust the future of the personal lines division to someone that no one wished to follow. Or would he?

Rita didn't take issue with anything I had to say, but she was clearly unmoved by my logic. From her vantage point, this wasn't a matter of Jerry choosing between good and evil. It was more a matter of choosing brawn over brains. For all its virtue, Ed Young's mild-mannered, Clark Kent demeanor betrayed his Superman talent. To know Ed was to love and admire him, but that wasn't good enough for Jerry in his successor.

Jerry wanted someone who resembled his image and likeness. Bob was the perfect match. Though no one ever accused Jerry of being the devil incarnate, both he and Bob could scare the bejesus out of you. But the most important trait that the two men held in common was their extensive background in sales. Jerry knew that he could count on Bob to remain loyal to growth initiatives, which in Jerry's mind was of the utmost importance.

Rita was well aware of my strained relationship with Bob. But since the two of them were on friendly terms, she promised to speak with him on my behalf in hopes that we could find a way to put our troubled past behind us.

It was a gracious yet risky move on Rita's part to share such highly classified insider information. In the course of looking out for my best interest, she exposed herself in a way that could have easily backfired on her. Had I shared with Ed Young the details of our conversation, it would have undoubtedly caused a nasty stir. Rita had been Ed's protégé early in her career. He often spoke of her in admiring terms, to the point where I thought they were kindred spirits.

Whether they were kindred spirits or not, Rita had long ago cast her lot with Jerry. And Jerry, according to Rita, was casting his lot with Bob. That meant Ed was the odd man out. Rita knew what was coming around the bend and was kind enough to give me an early warning. How I chose to handle that early warning was entirely up to me. And whether it was in time to pacify Bob Gary was entirely up to him. Oh, what a tangled web!

It grieved me deeply to keep Rita's secret from Ed, but not nearly as much as sucking up to Bob. True to her word, Rita had arranged for the two of us to meet privately to discuss ways and means for me to serve Bob's interests while still reporting to Ed. The extent to which Bob would have me help him grow the business was in conflict with Ed's profit goals. Keeping secrets from Ed was bad enough, but I was not about to stab him in the back.

I made up my mind to cast my lot with Ed and started sleeping better at night. Then, in August 1994, another wild card was thrown into the senior management mix that offered new possibilities. Allstate was in the final stages of making a clean break from Sears and becoming a publicly traded company. As a parting gift, Sears saw fit to give Allstate two of its highly regarded senior executives.

Ed Liddy and Tom Wilson joined Allstate's senior management staff, which came as a surprise to everyone. Neither of them had an insurance background, but they knew a lot about money. Ed Liddy was a former CFO at G. D. Searle during the days when Donald Rumsfeld was CEO. Prior to joining Allstate, he was the CFO at Sears.

According to legend, Ed had hopes of succeeding Ed Brennan as CEO at Sears but lost out to Arthur Martinez, who left Saks to take the job. Ed Liddy's move to Allstate was a rumored to be a consolation prize.

Tom Wilson was Ed Liddy's protégé at Sears. Legend had it that he was the mastermind behind the sale of the Sears Tower. No one was quite sure how Ed Liddy and Tom Wilson would fit within Allstate, but it was clear that they were now major players. What impact their presence would have on Jerry Choate was the subject of wild speculation. My only hope was that Ed Young would emerge from the senior management shuffle with a sweeter deal than Bob Gary.

That soon proved to be wishful thinking on my part. In the fall of 1994, Jerry Choate was named president of Allstate, Ed Liddy was named COO, Tom Wilson was named CFO, and Bob Gary was named president of personal lines, just as Rita had predicted. Ed Young was named president of a newly formed international division, which was a septic way of putting him out to pasture. And Bob Gary's first act in his new position was to flush my career down the toilet.

Now that Bob was president of personal lines, all the vice presidents reported directly to him. One by one, he summoned each to his office and gave them their new marching orders. When my turn came, he shook my hand for the first time in his life and asked me what it felt like to be in charge of a department that no longer existed. I told him it felt better than shaking his clammy hand.

At this point in our relationship, there was no reason for pretense. Product Administration was immediately disbanded, and I was left to find a job elsewhere in the organization. My options were severely limited, since the only expertise I had was rooted in the personal lines division. For all intents and purposes, I was a man without a country. But Bob's vain attempt to banish me from Allstate turned out to be a blessing in disguise.

The greatest challenge facing Jerry Choate as president was orchestrating a successful spin-off from Sears. Plans had been in the making for quite some time, and there was a tremendous amount of shareholder value at stake. Allstate stood on the threshold of closing a deal on the largest initial public offering in history to date, but the investment community had reason for pause.

In August 1992, Hurricane Andrew struck the southeastern tip of Florida. In less than half an hour, it managed to wipe out nearly one-third of Allstate's surplus—more than four billion dollars. In January 1994, the Northridge earthquake struck the San Fernando Valley of southern California. It measured 6.7 in magnitude and took less than twenty-five seconds to wipe out another billion dollars of surplus.

It had become quite apparent that Allstate was overexposed to catastrophic events that were occurring on a more frequent basis than one in a hundred years. (This was precisely the point we had tried to make a few years back as members of the now defunct property group!) Rating agencies like Standard & Poor's, Moody's, and A. M. Best were threatening to downgrade Allstate's credit rating, unless we could strike a better balance between premiums and exposure. Failure to do so would ruin our public offering.

As the newly appointed president of personal lines, it should have been Bob Gary's job to clean up this mess. But Jerry knew that Bob was a one-trick pony. All he thought to do was sell, sell, sell, which was the root cause of our problem. Knowing what needed to be done, and how to best go about it, was clearly a job for Superman. So while Jerry saw fit to give Bob the job of president, he gave the most critical part of Bob's job to Ed Young.

While settling into his new job as president of our newly formed international group, Ed put together a small, hard-hitting group that was known as the exposure management team. Given his actuarial expertise, John Drennan was chosen as team leader. The other members of the "cat team," as we were dubbed, included actuaries, lawyers, claims associates, and me.

Ed confided in me that there were two primary reasons for placing me on the team:

1) Bob Gary would have nothing to do with me, and
2) I had served him well in the past.

Once the assignment was completed, there would probably be nothing left for me to do.

For some strange reason, it didn't faze me in the least that I could soon be out of a job. If I had to guess, I'd say it was a function of God's work at hand. I still had my title, my corner office, and my pride. The nature of the cat team's work was at the center of Allstate's universe. As a leader within the insurance industry, major competitors were following our every move. No matter how grim my future prospects might have been, this felt like my shining moment.

Ed Young was also in his element, doing what he did best. Under his enlightened leadership, the cat team assessed the company's probable maximum loss, or PML, given the volume of business on our books exposed to catastrophic losses by way of hurricanes and earthquakes. That assessment was then put within the context of what the investment community considered an appropriate degree of risk in terms of shareholder interest.

In the final analysis, it was generally agreed that Allstate needed to shed one billion dollars' worth of property exposure in order to execute a successful IPO. Goldman

Sachs, lead underwriters of our public offering, was in complete agreement with this assessment. Unfortunately for us, that was the easiest part of solving our problem. The hardest part would be divesting exposure without violating state insurance laws, drying up vital revenue streams, and destroying the homeowners insurance market altogether.

It had taken several decades to write ourselves into this problem. We had less than a year to work our way out. The first thing we had to do was lobby the California and Florida state legislatures. Without swift and significant change to existing state laws and regulations, there would be no way to meet our goals. Luckily for us, these legislative bodies were already considering changes to existing codes in light of the recent havoc caused by hurricanes and earthquakes.

In January 1996, the California Earthquake Authority was formed. It was a publicly managed entity privately funded by participating property and casualty insurers. It allowed overexposed insurers like Allstate to retain customers at a base level of coverage. Companies could provide "no frills" mini policies at adjusted rates to maintain market stability.

The extent to which the CEA contained future loses was appreciable, but did very little in terms of reducing our overall exposure to catastrophic losses. My underwriting instincts led me to believe that the only way to achieve our billion-dollar mandate was to significantly reduce our customer base in the state of Florida. I felt that hurricanes posed the greatest risk to our financial strength given their regularity. Ever heard of earthquake season?

Neither Jerry Choate nor Bob Gary was comfortable with my idea. Given their sales instincts, they refused to believe what they knew to be true. Ed Young was ordered to search high and low for a way to reduce our exposure to hurricanes without affecting our customer base. Under normal market conditions, he might have been able to do just that by purchasing reinsurance.

Major reinsurers had serious reservations about taking on additional exposure to hurricanes. Ed Young was starting to believe that hurricanes were uninsurable events that could only to be redressed by the federal government, as it did with floods. Relief from the federal government required an act of Congress for which time constraints didn't allow. With traditional insurance options seemingly unavailable, Goldman Sachs started to explore unconventional investment strategies. As a member of the cat team, I was privy to some of the deliberations. It sounded like voodoo economics, witchcraft bullshit to me, the kind of stuff that probably led over time to the creation of collateralized debt obligation. Lord, have mercy.

While all of that was going on, I was hard at work putting a plan together with a noble assist from the reinsurance brokerage firm E. W. Blanche. A young upstart by the name of Rod Fox was the company's shooting star. Rather than deal with major reinsurers, Rod made contact with smaller players in the marketplace that might see this as a golden opportunity to exploit Allstate's gluttonous position.

Rod put me in contact with a gentleman by the name of Ralph Milo, who was president of a small insurance company located in midtown Manhattan. Ralph cobbled together a consortium of reinsurance providers that offered to take a billion dollars' worth of hurricane exposure off Allstate's books under extremely favorable conditions toward them.

Allstate would cede a portion of its Florida homeowner book of business to a Florida startup company, owned and operated by the consortium. Included in the mix of business was a billion dollars' worth of hurricane exposure, along with a considerable amount of highly profitable business located outside cat-prone areas, like Orlando and Tallahassee. In addition to ceding that business and its written premium, Allstate would pay Clarendon a bounty to address solvency issues, and a whole lot more.

This was not the kind of deal Allstate was used to making. It smacked of being extorted by pipsqueaks to whom it ordinarily wouldn't give the time of day, let alone its sacred treasure. Jerry Choate was appalled by the terms of the deal and made no bones about objecting to it. And since I was the one who had brought the deal to the table, you can imagine how Bob Gary felt. Ed Young was on board in a milquetoast way. The only one anxious to pull the trigger was Ed Liddy, against the better judgment of Tom Wilson.

The deal needed the approval of the Florida legislature as well as the Department of Insurance. Bill Nelson was Florida's Treasurer and Insurance Commissioner at the time. This was the same Bill Nelson who had served in the U.S. House of Representatives 1979–1991. During that time, Bill took a six-day trip through space on board the Space Shuttle *Columbia*. (Ten days after his safe return, the Space Shuttle *Challenger* exploded shortly after liftoff.) Elected in 2000, Bill currently serves in the U.S. Senate.

Legally, fiscally, and politically speaking, Bill Nelson was uniquely qualified to represent Florida's interests. While Jerry Choate and his staff continued nitpicking the Clarendon deal, Bill Nelson and his staff were doing much the same. Most of my time was now being spent coordinating a response to concerns being raised by Bill Nelson and his team. Ed Liddy was taking it upon himself to keep Jerry Choate in the fold.

Since I was in the position of playing Allstate's point guard on the deal, Ed Liddy would call me both at home and in the office to get an update on how things were going. He worried that Bill Nelson might not sign off on the deal, which I assured him was the least of my concerns. I reminded him of the tone being set in meetings with Jerry Choate, who, in the time that had passed since we started this process, was appointed CEO and chairman of Allstate. Ed Liddy succeeded Jerry as president, but my father's admonition that "jacks don't beat kings" was still very fresh in my mind.

During the first phone call Ed Liddy placed to my home, I confessed that I was uncomfortable advancing a proposal Jerry Choate vigorously opposed. Ed told me not to worry about it; he would handle Jerry. It was as if I was listening to a brand of heresy being spoken by Judas Iscariot. I knew Ed Liddy to be a bullet-sharp businessman, but there was something slightly untoward about what I heard him say. I hung up the phone and prayed to God that I hadn't become part of some wicked conspiracy.

After nearly twelve months of negotiations, we begrudgingly closed the deal. The Florida Hurricane Catastrophe Fund was amended in 1995. Florida was awarded IRS tax exemptions, Allstate was given approval to transfer a billion dollars of hurricane risk, Goldman Sachs moved forward with our record-breaking IPO, and Clarendon laughed all the way to the bank. In recognition of the role I had played in making all things possible, I managed to keep a job. Bob Gary was fit to be tied.

The cat team's work had only just begun. It took several more years to get a good handle on our hurricane exposure in places like the Gulf of Mexico and the eastern seaboard coastline. Had we not taken proper cues from Andrew, Hurricane Rita would have totally blown us away. Alas, the only thing soon to be "blowin' in the wind" at Allstate was my time as a productive member of the "Nifty Fifty."

When the cat team's work was done, I got what appeared to be a new lease on life. I went to work for Ron McNeil, a personal lines senior vice president with whom I had good relations. Ron reported to directly to Bob Gary, who was still very much determined to run me out of town on a rail. But Jerry Choate was kind enough to intercede on my behalf and afforded Ron the latitude to use me as he saw fit.

With Bob effectively held at bay, Ron put me in charge of a small marketing team. Our mission was to explore new opportunities that might increase Allstate's market share. Once again, bright ideas were met with senior management apathy, and, in Bob Gary's case, outright disgust. Whether it was urban marketing, affinity marketing, or product development, everything we ran up the flagpole came back down shot full of holes.

Another senior vice president named Mick McCabe would eventually head Allstate's marketing campaign. Mick and I were on friendly terms, thanks to his close personal relationship with Ed Young. My dear friend Ed had retired by now, but his memory lingered on. As a courtesy to Ed, more than anything else, Mick encouraged me to keep my pipe dreams alive. Rather than going through the process of running more ideas up the flagpole, I decided to go straight to the top.

The year was 1999. Ed Liddy had replaced Jerry Choate as CEO. Several years had passed since the Clarendon deal, but I was hoping Mr. Liddy would remember the key role I had played in resolving Allstate's billion-dollar dilemma. Back in those days, Ed Liddy and I had routinely talked on the phone, and although we hadn't done so lately, it didn't strike me as out of the ordinary to call him and seek some of his time. Apparently, I was wrong.

All I wanted from Ed Liddy was his reaction to my master policy concept. If the new CEO showed the slightest bit of interest in the idea, then others in senior management might have been inclined to show some as well. But I never got the chance to speak with Ed Liddy. Instead of returning my call, Mr. Liddy called Mick. He instructed Mick to contact me and find out why I was calling him. Apparently, after the Clarendon deal was done, Mr. Liddy had no use for my bright ideas. He was never a mentor or sponsor of mine, and obviously had no intent of ever becoming one. I can only assume that I wasn't his kind of guy. When Mick came to my office and asked me what was up, I knew the end was nigh.

I remember my last day on the job like it was yesterday, and for the record, it sucked more than my first. Gone forever were the heady days of scaling the corporate ladder, the exhilarating thrill of it all, and the attendant financial windfalls. But after more than twenty-seven years of working hard for the money, I no longer had to work to live. As far as a rewarding career is concerned, I'd say I got my money's worth.

CLOSE

Mine is the story of a snotty-nosed kid, born and raised in Harlem, who went on to enjoy a rewarding career in a place called Corporate America. I attribute my good fortune to a whole host of things, not the least of which were timing and dumb luck. But what mattered most, in terms of my success, were the blessings bestowed upon me early on in life.

Perhaps the greatest blessing of all was nourishment from a nuclear family unit that included loving parents and an older brother. Collectively, they instilled me with a sense of pride, self-esteem, and a license to challenge life with gusto. And there was no better place to learn hard life lessons than on the mean streets of New York City.

Moving from one street corner to another often required me to confront difficult situations. Over time, I developed a sixth sense and personal courage that rendered me streetwise, perceptive, and comfortable with change. I also grew to be ambitious, industrious, and unafraid of failure. I was willing to take intelligent risks, let the chips fall where they may, and live with the consequences. "Never let them see you sweat" were words I came to live by.

This sort of bravado would serve me well in Corporate America, along with several other gifts. My formal education in elementary and high school provided me with morals, ethics, and technical skills that allowed me to distinguish myself. During my days at Morehouse College, I came under the philosophical influence of Dr. Martin Luther King Jr. If you've ever listened to his "I Have a Dream" speech, it should be easy to understand why.

By the time I had my liberal arts degree in hand, I was ready, if not anxious, to find a job. And that's when Allstate proved to be a blessing. As a burgeoning giant in the insurance industry, Allstate was financially strong and geared toward growth, with a nurturing corporate culture. Employees enjoyed a comfortable work environment where they could hold down a steady job or aggressively pursue a management career, depending on their skills and interest. They also had access to generous employee benefits like group health insurance, profit sharing programs, 401K programs, and continuing education.

These are standard measures for a great American company, which Allstate was, then and now. And if you find the need to work in Corporate America, you would be wise to join forces with a company of equal measure. Regardless of your background, skills, and abilities, if you work for a company that doesn't aspire to be great, I doubt that you will ever find success.

I also seriously doubt that you will find success unless you embrace the corporate culture, study the business you're in, engage in corporate politics, kiss a little ass, build a network of mentors and sponsors, "love" your bosses, take intelligent risks, work hard, be patient, learn from your mistakes, commit to solving problems, and help the company make money. All this, along with a little luck, should put you in good stead.

Godspeed and good luck in your career pursuits! May your monsters be tamed, your mentors plentiful, and your sponsors everlasting. Amen.

8240348R0

Made in the USA
Lexington, KY
21 January 2011